*To Karyl —
May laughter always be
a part of your day!
Dan Brennan*

OBSERVATIONS FROM THE CHURCH OFFICE

Dan Brennan

**Original Illustrations by
Jorner**

OBSERVATIONS FROM THE CHURCH OFFICE

I asked, "Does God have a sense of humor?"
God said, "Have you looked in the mirror?"

Dan is a member of the Christian Comedy Association which is an association of Christians committed to offering faith affirming truth through the craft of comedy.

Notice: Churches have permission to reproduce any of these "observations" for use in their newsletters or bulletins. Please provide appropriate credit to the author

If you have questions: email: dan@danscomedy.com

Copyright © 2015 Dan Brennan

Table of Contents

Introduction 7
A Chorus of Crickets 9
Going Solar 10
The "Eyes" Have it 11
The Tell-Tale Vase 12
Answering the Call for Help 13
Humbug! 14
Other Duties as Assigned… 16
Milestones or Millstones? 17
Sounds of the Season? 19
Saving Christmas Morning
   a Guide for Foolish Husbands 21
My Name is Dan and I'm a Technology Addict 23
Ballin the Jack 25
PBK on Speed Dial 27
Headbanging Seems So Painful 29
It is What it is. Or Is it? 31
Wherein Dan's position in the pecking order of life is made
   perfectly clear 33
Dan is told to "Go fly a kite!" 35
Resisting Temptation 37
A rose by any other name might be pastrami 39
Does God Shop at Wal-Mart?
   Small Miracle in a Big Box Store 41
Too Much Love...Or, Is That Really Your Desktop Background? ..43
Spending Mother's Day in the Bathroom 45
Making Music - It's the Human Thing to Do. 47

Render unto Caesar that which is Caesar's
or, A Tale of Two Salads 49
Who Am I? 51
Babbling as an Art Form 53
Through the Rear View Mirror 55
My New Best Friends 59
Toto - I have a feeling we're not in Kansas anymore 61
It Isn't Easy Being Green 63
Prayer in Unexpected Places 65
Where's a Man to Go? 67
Learning the Sign Language of McDonalds 69
What's a guy have to do to shop in peace in quiet? 71
Babies are just miniature women in onesies. 73
The Secret War to End Haggling 75
When Good Recliners Go Bad 77
No Appointment Necessary 80
Creating the Perfect "Stuffy" 82
Have You Spoken to Your Cashier Lately? 84
Rolling the Pumpkins 86
My Binders Runneth Over 88
It was a dark and stormy night… 90
But honey, I'm saving money… 92
How Do You Stuff a Tofurkey? 94
The Perils of Gift Buying 96
Are we there yet? 98
Exchanging of the Gifts - or Regifting Revisited 100
Defying the Laws of Aging 102

An aging shopper recalls the battle cry, "Remember the Cabbage Patch Kids"..104
The Good Old Days? 106
The Right Place at the Right Time 108
Resisting the Lure of Heavy Equipment 109
Please answer your secret security question 111
Did Jesus Lip-Synch the Sermon on the Mount 113
Famous Last Words: "I think I'll just get her a card." 115
The Day the Earth Stood Still (or at least Southern Maryland)..117
Watching Paint Dry 119
The Real MasterCard...121
The Undiscovered Easter Egg...123
Dan wants to kill Jiminy Cricket....................................125
Dan Goes to the Circus 127
Dan longs to look like his caricature 129
The Uncomfortable Intrusions of Social Media...........131
An Indispensable Tool for Dieting 133
Warning! Warning! Geek Alert!
    Content May Not Be of Interest to Normal People..............**135**
Remembering Mom in the Checkout Lane...................137
Dan Discovers The Root of All Evil...............................139
Remember the Date? 141
Heckling as an Art Form...143
A Square Peg, a Round Hole and Me 145
Dressing for Success 147
Multitasking - Not Always a Good Thing.....................149
Memory - all alone in the moonlight…........................151
Some Assembly Required 153

What Would You Do? 155
Patience is a virtue - at least my wife says it is 157
"The Better to See You With, My Dear" 159
How many pairs of glasses does it take to change a light bulb? ...161
Apology Not Accepted 163
Thinking Clearly? 165
And the Survey Says… 167
Where Are the Opposable Thumbs? 169
 Hurry Up and Wait! 171
Which Way is Up? 173
Dan learns that "fixing" isn't all it's cracked up to be. 174
The Day the Music Died 175
My Dog Went to the Maryland DogFest, and All I Got Was…...177
Blazing Sun, Flip Flops, Chlorine - Not Quite Heaven 179
Greater love hath no man than this, that he should peel a hard boiled egg for his wife. 181
Where Have All the Neckties Gone? 183
Nature to Dan: "Drop the camera, step away from
      the woods and no one will get hurt!" 185
Is this medication right for me? 187

Introduction

The license plate on my Buick La Crosse (yes, I'm that old) reads "I GOT JOY". I borrowed it from one of my favorite Christian songs 'I've Got Joy", which I use to open many of my comedy gigs. It's a constant reminder for me that the joy which comes from God is something the world can never take away.

But, you say, the world is a nasty place. War, hunger, poverty, crime are all around us. Yes, that's true, but God gave us a unique gift. He gave us the ability to laugh. No other creature can do that. And laughter is a powerful tool in our daily battle with life's trials and tribulations. I have a plaque hanging on my wall that says it very well: "Trouble knocked on the door, but hearing laughter, hurried away." That's a quote from one of America's earliest humorists, Benjamin Franklin.

As a part-time, aspiring, struggling, yet to be discovered stand-up comedian, I'm accustomed to looking for humor in everyday situations. I think that's what sets us comedians apart from regular folks. We are able to see the funny side of life as it takes its daily poke at us.

But what I didn't know was that God is often using those daily experiences to speak to us. God's wisdom can be found everywhere. We just need to look for it. I'm convinced that God is often poking me through life's little oddities.

The pages that follow are taken from my weekly efforts to share my "observations" with the congregation of Peace Lutheran Church in Waldorf, Maryland. The columns were part of the Sunday Bulletin provided for worship services. This book is not intended as a daily devotional, but as, perhaps, a way to start or finish your day with a smile.

I hope you enjoy reading them as much as I have enjoyed writing them.

Is God poking you?

Dan Brennan

A Chorus of Crickets

As a sometimes comedian, I am very much aware of the most terrifying sound in the world to those standing on a stage with a microphone. No, it's not the hecklers in the back row (and no, I'm not referring to the pastor, here). The most terrifying sound to a comedian is silence, often depicted by the plaintive cry of crickets chirping in the background.

The church office recently endured a small invasion by the little critters (they're gone now), but I couldn't help but notice them in the otherwise quietude that is the office early in the morning. I wanted them to be gone, not because they frightened me, but because they had invaded the time I most enjoy. Early in the morning, before the day's events have really begun, is the time when I can enjoy the value that silence can bring; the opportunity to be alone with my thoughts except for the Lord who shares all of my thoughts all of the time. It's a chance to speak to Him freely, and, yes, to joke with Him as well.

Did you know that God has a wonderful sense of humor? Well, He does. He and I were sharing some thoughts just the other morning, and I gave Him a few lines from a new routine I'm working on, and suddenly, there they were, the crickets. Do you think God was trying to tell me something?

And now, if you'll excuse me, the exterminator is at the door.

Going Solar

I recently purchased a solar powered wireless keyboard. Why? Well, to be honest, mostly because I enjoy the latest electronic gadgets, and not so much because I'm overly concerned with saving energy. What's interesting about this particular keyboard is that it can store power not only from the energy of daylight, but from normal office or room lighting as well, and, I am told, as little as two hours exposure to light is sufficient to insure continued service for as long as two months in total darkness.

I got to thinking. If the power produced by one simple light bulb can provide life giving force for two months in the darkness, how much greater must the power provided to each of us by the Light of the World be to see us through our trials. Jesus is the Light of our World, and we are empowered by his energy to see our way through the darkest days of our lives. And unlike man-made sources, His light will not fail us ever.

And now, if you'll excuse me, I need to explain to my wife that I bought this expensive keyboard in order illustrate an important lesson in faith. Prayers will be needed.

The "Eyes" Have it

I've reached that unfortunate age where my ears, nerves, and general sensibilities are easily disturbed. I'm one of those who cringe in horror while standing in the checkout lane of the supermarket when a mother with one or more cranky children joins the line. It's hard to decide on the Hershey bar with almonds, vs. the plain when your brain is scrambled by a wailing infant.

So imagine my trepidation this past Sunday, while sitting quietly in church minding my own business, a family with an infant sat down in the pew just in front of me. The child was encapsulated very comfortably in a car seat/carrier which when placed on the pew resulted in the infant

positioned so that he and I were staring eye to eye. Okay, yes, he was very cute. There, I said it. Still, I was anticipating the inevitable crying to begin anytime.

As I sat there with my preconceived notions about how he was going to behave and what he might do, I realized that he was looking at me completely without judgment of any kind. To his eyes, I was just another person. He saw me without my flaws and was ready to accept me as I was. I wonder what it would be like if all of us could see the world the way that infant does? I wonder what God would think of us if we did?

And now, if you'll excuse me, there's a two for one deal on Hershey bars at the grocery store.

The Tell-Tale Vase

Nobody tells me nuttin'! OK, so my English ain't so good, but hey, I'm just repeating what I hear so often from members of the church. It's a common refrain often preceded by such statements as "I didn't know that was going on" or "Why didn't someone tell me about that? or "I don't know where to find ____ (insert your own noun here).

For some of us being in the dark is a normal condition. My wife has long given up on hoping that I will remember all the little details of our first date, our wedding (I know we had one), our kids' names (ok, I'm exaggerating that one a little), and where I put my car keys. So I try to counter that problem by surrounding myself with helpful hints. One of my wife's aunts was kind enough to give us a ceramic crock with the date of our wedding etched into the front. It sits proudly in our kitchen holding various wooden spoons. But its real function is to allow me to recall our wedding anniversary with just a quick glance. Of course my wife always asks that inevitable follow-up question: "How many years?" Then my new family's unintended curse kicks in. Seems the aunt put the wrong year on the crock. It's off by one and I can never remember whether it's one short or one over. I guess wrong every time.

Still, I wonder how church members can be "in the dark" when there are so many ways for us to keep up with what's happening at Peace. You're reading one of them now. Lots of announcements here. How about the monthly newsletter? Announcements on Sunday morning are yet another way as are the many fliers on the tables in the Narthex. Sometimes e-mail is used to share important information. Do you check your mailbox regularly? Oh, and did I forget to mention the church website? Tons of great information, forms, and other goodies can be found there.

So, I know what I'm going to be doing this afternoon. I'll be perusing the bulletin, checking the website, reading my e-mail, reviewing back issues of the newsletter, oh, and one more thing, that vase.

And now, if you'll excuse me, I'll be using a black magic marker to once and for all end the curse of the misprinted vase. Take that, mother-in-law.

Answering the Call for Help

The phone rang. I answered it. It was another request for food or financial assistance. I was annoyed. Maybe it was because I had spent the previous night fielding one call after another from this charity or that company wanting me to support their cause or buy their product. Maybe it was because on my way to work I had passed one or two people on street corners sporting signs asking for money. Maybe it was the trash can overflowing with junk mail. It seems that everywhere we go, whatever we do, we are constantly feeling pressure to "help".

I was feeling a bit like old Ebenezer Scrooge (shameless self-promotion here as I will be playing the Ghost of Christmas Present in the local community theater production of "A Christmas Carol".) And so I prayed. And as I was asking the Lord to deliver me from requests for help, it suddenly occurred to me that I, myself, was asking for help.

Imagine what it must have been like for Jesus. Everywhere he went he was pestered by people wanting assistance, a hand out, a cure, etc. There was no "do not call" list available in His time. He couldn't opt out of receiving petitions for help and assistance. He couldn't just turn up the volume on his IPOD and ignore the constant pleas of the needy. And right to this very day He is still listening to our pleas for help. And what's more, answering them.

I can't help everyone, but I can always offer an ear to listen, a shoulder to lean on, a word of encouragement, and a shared prayer to help someone direct their request to the one who can answer their need, Jesus. And I can be thankful that I have been blessed to have the good fortune I enjoy.

And so, at the end of the day, if we cannot do anything else, we can, as Tiny Tim, the Cratchits and even old Scrooge did, say, "God bless us, everyone!" I think He will.

And now, if you'll excuse me, I've got a few calls to answer.

Humbug!

I have it on good authority that Ebenezer Scrooge has for many years been the victim of unsubstantiated rumors that he despised Christmas. All because he was one day heard to scream loudly in the privacy of his own counting house, "HUMBUG!" What was not reported was the somewhat softer sound of a "squish" as he dropped his foot onto the scampering insect. Yes, the Humbug is a rare species of beetle from the rain forests of South America. But that didn't matter. A disgruntled clerk named Cratchit leaked the story to the local press. It was picked up by a writer of some repute, and the rest, as they say, is history.

It's very easy to misinterpret something we overhear, especially when we don't have the benefit of the full context of the conversation. We humans are uniquely capable of jumping to conclusions based on the slimmest evidence. As a child I continually tried to divine what my Christmas presents would be by listening in on my parents' conversations at night. I was disappointed every Christmas when my new bike became a pair of snow boots and a hooded jacket. In Junior High School I frequently misinterpreted an innocent smile from an attractive girl as meaning she was in love with me. I didn't get a lot of dates. Sitting in the church office, I "overhear" a lot of conversations, but usually only bits and pieces. It has the potential for creating a lot of those situations they refer to when they say a "little knowledge is a dangerous thing." Fortunately, I have a short memory.

    I think Jesus would have sat down with Ebenezer and had a long talk before pronouncing him a curmudgeon (a term I've heard the pastor here use in passing reference to someone in the office.) Jesus would have wanted all the facts before presuming to draw a conclusion. And it's probably good advice for the rest of us as well.

    And now if you'll excuse me, I've got a bug to stomp.

Other Duties as Assigned...

I remember thinking to myself as I was preparing for my interview with Peace Lutheran Church for the coveted position of Administrative Assistant, "Looks like a simple enough job. Do a few bulletins, file a few papers, answer a few phone calls. No stress, no worries." I even remember reviewing the job description (my lawyer was out of town, but I managed). No surprises there, although I might have asked a few questions about that ubiquitous phrase common to many job descriptions, "Other duties as assigned." I was mostly right. The most common tasks I deal with are pretty routine, and it's easy to budget my time and resources. But oh those other duties - they sure can disrupt my plans.

Turns out though, that the activities I hadn't necessarily bargained for often are the most interesting and rewarding. Now don't get me wrong, I'm not talking about the news that a toilet is running in the ladies room, or the roof is leaking. My membership in the "Home Handyman Club" was revoked years ago due to incompetence with tools. But there are so many little projects here at Peace that allow me to utilize the skills that the good Lord has given me and which provide me with a sense of satisfaction that the "assigned" duties never could. Whether it's helping to prepare content for the new Narthex display, or designing a flier, card, or other announcement, or perhaps helping someone to resolve a problem with a church-related issue, I usually leave the office feeling pretty good about the day.

All of us have our jobs, the things we get paid to do. But in accepting His gifts of skills or talents, we agree to God's fine print to use them not only in our daily work, but in "other duties as assigned." There are many ways to meet that obligation. Whatever your gift, whatever you love to do, there is a need for that skill in your church. Don't miss out on a chance to feel pretty good about your day.

And now, if you'll excuse me, I just know there's a toilet running out of control somewhere in the building.

Milestones or Millstones?

Life is filled with events that mark major changes in our lives. We often call these events milestones. Some we look forward to such as receiving our driver's license, finishing school, getting married, while others not so much. This year my life was rudely interrupted by two of those "not so much" moments. In July I received my Medicare card, followed in a few days by an invitation to "like" the Scooter Store on Facebook. I was expecting a call from Wilford Brimley with an offer for free diabetes test strips at any moment.

So there I am on my birthday flipping through the Scooter Store brochure, and armed with the knowledge that I can now get my colon tested free, if I can just manage to get my walker assembled and shuffle out to the car. It was a little humbling to say the least.

But you know, as I was feeling sorry for my aging condition, and contemplating the possibility of cutting off any future mail deliveries, it occurred to me that there were an awful lot of things that I had not gotten in the mail. I had not received a notice from my Doctor's office telling me the test results from my recent physical showed a serious illness. I had not received a foreclosure notice from my mortgage holder. I did not receive a letter from a family member informing me of the loss of a loved one. And although I did receive a notice that the warranty on my washing machine was expiring, that was the worst.

In short, all that had really happened was that I was moving into a new phase of a life that has been filled with many blessings. So I was a little older. So I was a little less mobile that I might have been 25 years ago. I had cable television, a car, a great wife, wonderful friends, a digital camera and a sense of humor. A lot to be thankful for. So I thank the good Lord for taking care of me up till now, and I trust He will continue to do the same for me in the future. I guess I'll leave the mail delivery alone.

And now, if you'll excuse me, I've got to finish my Christmas list; there's a racy looking red scooter on page 3 of the brochure, and if I call right now, I can get free shipping.

Sounds of the Season?

It was a cool, crisp Saturday morning; a day I had been anticipating for many weeks. It would be the first time in a long while that I did not have to be somewhere early in the morning. The warmth of the blankets and the softness of the pillow were calling my name longingly. That's when it happened. The quiet of the morning was shattered by what I was sure had been a passing jet plane. The whine of the engine convinced me the plane was on its way to a crash landing in my backyard. I tried in vain to muffle the sound by ducking beneath the covers and throwing the pillow over my

head. But the noise would not be denied. It grew louder and louder, then softer, then louder again. I felt a bit like the Grinch being assaulted by the incessant singing of the Whoville Whos. "Oh, The Noise, Noise, Noise, Noise!".

I sprang from my bed to see what was the matter. It was near freezing outside as I peered through the front window, but all I could see was a

19

strange little figure wrapped head to toe for warmth, and sporting what appeared to be massive headphones. Looking a bit like a "punk" Santa Claus, he had a "pack upon his back", but I soon learned it was not loaded with toys. No, it was that dreaded denizen of all suburban neighborhoods, the Gas Powered Leaf Blower. Wielding it like a medieval instrument of torture, he roamed back and forth, up and down, and around the sides of his house spewing forth its illegal level of mind blowing decibels. Why do you suppose it never occurs to someone that a device that requires you to wear protective ear gear might just be disturbing to the rest of humanity?

Now my neighbor isn't a terrible person, in fact, he and his wife are quite nice. Nor is the one on the other side of the woods behind me, the one who fires up his Hummer sized riding lawn mower every other day and merrily rides for hours with his headphones on. I think it's just another sign of our times. We all become so involved in our own world that we rarely consider the effect we may be having on others. If we stopped to think about it, we might act differently. We're not alone in the world, and we need to consider the needs and comforts of others, particularly at this time of the year.

I do admit to having to wipe a slight smirk from my face as I watch my neighbors work so tirelessly at getting rid of those leaves. Neighbor A blows his leaves onto Neighbor B's yard, where the wind promptly shifts them back to Neighbor A's yard. My leaves? Hey, I'm a nature lover, I like to leave them right where the Good Lord dropped them. It's winter folks. Put the power tools away and go back to bed.

Now if you'll excuse me, I need to get down to Lowes. There's a sale on rakes, and I've got a lot of neighbors to buy gifts for.

Saving Christmas Morning a Guide for Foolish Husbands

I awoke rather abruptly this morning, in a cold sweat, and trembling just a bit. I knew there was Christmas shopping to be done, and I had found myself drifting back to a year (that shall never be mentioned), when I had made that most fatal of husbandly errors. That year (the one I can't mention) I believed my wife. I asked her what she wanted for Christmas, and she looked me dreamily in the eyes and said, "Oh honey, don't get me anything. I have you and that's all I need." I believed her, and I smiled. I don't know whether it was because I was flattered, or because I stupidly thought I was off the hook for a present that year (the one I can't talk about).

Regardless, that Christmas morning when I appeared in a robe with a red ribbon and green bow in my hair, offering her a cup of hot chocolate and nothing more, things did not go well. While in the bathroom scraping the marshmallow out of my hair, I happened to see my salvation sitting in

the magazine rack. It was a catalog from Norwegian Cruise Lines (oh why did I throw out that Hickory Farms catalog?) I carefully tore a picture of a ship docked just off the coast of some unknown destination, and, while she was refilling her hot chocolate, dashed down to my office for the Christmas card (yes I had thought to get one of those), signed the card, stuck the picture inside, sealed it and went back upstairs. Who knew you could book a cruise on Christmas Day?

Christmas was saved! I had saved the day, not with finesse and planning, but thorough a stroke of dumb luck and a credit card. But then, that's the nature of men isn't it? We stumble along, often with the best intentions, making mistake after mistake, and generally trying to rectify those mistakes at the last minute with extravagant gifts. Perhaps there is a better way.

God, the founder of the first Christmas day, provided the true path to salvation, not just for one day, but for all time and for all people. And he didn't do it through dumb luck and a credit card. God saved the day for all of us by planning the most generous gift that has ever been given, the gift of his Son, Jesus Christ. Jesus didn't come from a catalog, or an online store, or a big box retailer, he came from the heart of the Father who loved us so much that he was willing to sacrifice his own Son. Now that's a gift you just can't beat.

Even men can learn and change. And so this Christmas, I will have a few gifts for my lovely wife, and among them will be a huge hug with thanks to God for sending her to me, and for sharing his Son with all of us.

And now if you will excuse me, I need to check the catalogs in the bathroom magazine rack. I need to make sure that the "Gifts under $50.00" catalog is front and center just in case.

My Name is Dan and I'm a Technology Addict

My church is home to several different groups dedicated to helping individuals cope with addictions, but there isn't yet one that can help me. You see, I'm addicted to technology. There I've said it, and I know that's the first step towards dealing with my problem. Trouble is, I don't know what the second step is. My office at home looks like the auxiliary warehouse for Best Buy, and my wife refuses to maintain my inventory of remote controls. Although I would never dream of getting up in the middle of the night for Black Friday deals, I'm the guy you might see in line at 3 a.m. waiting for the latest release of Windows, or desperately bidding on E-Bay for the last iPhone in the country.

If it's new, if it has buttons, and especially if it beeps, then I've got to have it. I'm so addicted that I have been identified as one of only 5 individuals in the entire country who reads owner's manuals. I do. I love them. There's something about delving into the inner workings of gadgets that fascinates me. As an addict you develop certain skills. For example, my latest acquisition was a Harmony Universal Remote Control. In order to purchase this without incurring the lasting wrath of my wife, I had to "skillfully" convince her that this was for her own good. I explained how it would replace six remotes we currently use. "Look," I told her, "you just have to push one button to watch a DVD." Apparently I managed to push her "button" because the next thing I knew, she was tearing up the owner's manual and threatening to hold a Tupperware party.

 I was online immediately downloading a replacement copy of the Harmony manual, and looking for some help for my addiction. I found one site that said it could cure me in a week. All I had to do was purchase and download their application which would only run on a tiny little device with buttons they were selling for $25.00. OK, OK, I'm not crazy, I didn't buy it…but if it had come in white?

 Lent is coming soon, and I need to give something up. I've already resolved to block the Wi-Fi signal to the master bathroom. Hey, it's a start.

 And now, if you'll excuse me, I've got an owner's manual for next year's iPhone to download and read, and Windows 8 is coming!

Ballin the Jack

I'm not sure why, but the period right after Christmas seems to be the preferred time for those annual events known as "Talent Shows." My church is staging their 3rd annual show this year.

Each year, as talent show time approaches, I receive a call from a good friend of mine asking, "Well, what are we going to do this year?" I confess to sighing just a little when the call comes. It's not that I don't want to do something with him, it's just that being a stand-up comic, my preferred performance mode is to work alone. I admit to being much more comfortable that way. I think it's the control thing. When you work alone you don't need to be dependent on anyone but yourself. You don't have to worry about the other guy knowing his part, or missing a cue, or maybe getting sick at the last minute. And maybe even more basic, when you write something for someone else you open yourself up to criticism, suggested changes, and somebody messing with "your stuff."

Imagine, for example, that I asked the pastor to write a sermon that we could deliver together (OK, I know I'm dreaming here). He writes this brilliant work of art, shows it to me, and I immediately begin to outline how it could be "better" if he would just do this, or that, or change that word to this one, maybe drop that illustration, and, oh, don't tell that old joke. Wonder how that would go?

Actually, that fear of rejection of my work happened this year. I shared with my friend my idea and a prototype for an "Interview with a Curmudgeon". It was going to be an interview with Ebenezer Scrooge in which he got to tell his side of the story. I had thought about it for months, gotten a lot of it written, and then shared it with my friend. Now John is not the type of guy to mince words. He told me, "It stinks. It's not funny." As I was crossing John off of next year's Christmas list, I found myself looking more objectively at the script. He was right. It wasn't funny - OK, it stinks.

And so, there I was, the pressure was on. John and I had done some very funny stuff over the past two shows, and I didn't want to let him down. As I sat there wondering what to do next, I found myself inexplicably humming a catchy little tune from 1942 called "Ballin the Jack". You remember, "First you put your two knees close up tight. Then you swing 'em to the left then you swing 'em to the right." The natural fit for that song, I knew immediately was the local cable company (I know you're just dying to know what they have to do with each other.) A new skit was born, and John and I will bring the house down.

Sometimes God wants us to work alone, but just as often he pairs us with another to help us find direction and purpose. It's easy to resist the help of others or see it as interference, but I'm grateful for John, and for a kooky song and dance that helped me uncover a better, more entertaining path for this year's show.

And now if you'll excuse me, I only have a couple of weeks to teach John to "twist around, twist around with all of his might."

PBK on Speed Dial

Did you know you can pay as much for a mattress for a baby's crib as you might for a king size bed? Did you know that sheets for that mattress are apparently as expensive to make as those for your king size bed? These and other rude awakenings have been thrust open me lately as I accompany my wife on shopping trips for gifts for my daughter's baby shower.

Now my experience with baby showers extends as far as telling my wife to have a good time, and enjoying a few hours alone with the TV while she plays games, and exchanges oohs and ahhs with other like-minded women while eating tiny sandwiches and sipping tea. That is to say: never been to one.

Well apparently while I was enjoying TV, the 21st century arrived and the concept of co-ed baby showers became the order of the day. Suddenly I was embroiled in discussions about invitations, what food to have, where to house the relatives (husbands and all) who would be coming from out of town, how to modify inane party games to accommodate male players and more I cannot mention.

The baby shower has now turned into an all-day affair complete with dinner for the entire family, accommodations for a small army and more chicken salad sandwiches than I could ever have imagined.

And so this past Saturday I found myself in a strange land known as PBK (Pottery Barn Kids). What, I wondered, did kids want with pottery? But there was no pottery, only exorbitantly priced baby furniture and more pregnant women than should ever have been in one place. Did you know you could have a cast made of your belly? I'm trying to get rid of mine, and others are making casts of theirs - outrageous.

The cost of all of this was starting to depress me. But that changed. Our next stop was a place called "Baby to Be Images". My daughter was having a 3D/4D imaging session. I've seen ultrasounds of babies, but I wasn't prepared for this. To see the actual face, hands, and feet of my granddaughter live and with such great clarity; to see her eyes open and close, her hand move to cover her mouth, her lips seem to actually appear to be blowing a kiss to us was beyond awesome. And then, I could swear, she smiled! And that was my undoing.

From that moment on I knew that no mattress would ever be good enough, no sheet soft enough, and certainly no baby shower worthy of that beautiful bundle of God's blessings. I've got PBK on speed dial. Bring on those party games!

And now if you'll excuse me, I've got to go. The plaster of paris on my tummy is just about dry.

Headbanging Seems So Painful

A few weeks ago I mentioned an old, old song, "Ballin the Jack". As it turns out it is just one of many old, old songs I have a tendency to hum, sing, and/or mangle from time to time. And like most people in my age category (not as old as dirt, but definitely senior to dust and lint), I often lament how few members of the younger generation recognize or appreciate those old chestnuts. I have this fear that at some point the tunes will be forgotten entirely, or worse, I'll be singing them one day and someone will have me committed for senility.

But as I was contemplating this woeful lack of musical diversity among younger folks, it occurred to me that I couldn't identify 99% of the songs that are on today's top 10 charts (do they still have those?) I sometimes enjoy watching "American Idol" (OK, yes, mostly for the bad auditions), but the reality is I hardly ever recognize the songs being sung. It seems that I don't allow much diversity into my musical world either. I was visiting my wife's family recently, and one of her nieces had married a musician who called himself a "headbanger." Here's the Wikipedia definition of the term: "Headbanging is a type of dance which involves violently shaking the head in time with the music, most commonly in the rock, punk and heavy metal music genres." He asked me if I wanted to see a sample of one of his performances which he had videotaped on his smart phone. After watching I said, "Well you know, I can't really tell if I like the music because of all the noise." There was a period of awkward silence. "Oh, I said, you mean that was the music?"

I wonder if it's fair to criticize the younger generation for not embracing our music if we are not willing to at least familiarize ourselves with theirs? Now to be clear, I'm not suggesting that some of us more mature types will ever learn to love hard rock or rap, or even manage to understand the lyrics of most of today's musical hits, but surely there are a few gems out there that are worth listening to. It's probably helpful to remember that even in what we might think of as the golden age of music, there were a lot of really bad songs produced. Take the first line of the memorable "Hut Sut" song from the 1940's: *Hut-Sut Rawlson on the rillerah and a brawla, brawla sooit.* Try explaining that one to the kids. (Aside note: that line caused my spell checker to implode.)

Music is, in the end, a lot like life. As we go through life we encounter an awful lot that we should simply ignore, but hidden among the mundane things we experience each day are bits of God's wonderful works. To discover them we sometimes have to be willing to dig through the barriers that we ourselves erect. Let's help our kids appreciate the music we love, and at the same time give them a chance to share the best of their world with us.

And now if you'll excuse me I've got to get back to learning the second line of the "Hut Sut" song, I'll be singing it at a headbanger's concert this weekend.

It is What it is. Or Is it?

I'm not sure what has happened to the English language, or perhaps more accurately, our ability to communicate in complete sentences. Now the wonderful group of people who proof my production of the bulletin each week, especially this column, are probably wondering what I, of all people, am doing critiquing communication issues, but our growing dependence on annoying phrases or shorthand, is driving me crazy.

Been to a restaurant lately? Did you know that asking for extra napkins, or a soda refill was "No Problem"? Wow, that's such a relief. I had worried all day long that my presence there to order a meal might be a problem. And when the check arrived, I found myself saying "Thank you", to the server, even though it should have been the other way around. I can't even remember the last time a clerk or check-out person thanked me. "Help with carrying your bags out, grandpa" was the closest I've gotten.

Ever caught someone in a mistake, or had a drink spilled by a passing stranger, or any other inconvenience caused by someone else's inattention? "My bad" is the standard response. No real acceptance of accountability or

"Mom, it is what it is."

genuine regret for the act. Just "My bad." Again, I'm relieved to know that at least it wasn't, my bad.

But then, "whatever", as they say. It is what it is. Or is it? In the lexicon of obnoxious 21st century phrases the most annoying, at least to me, has to be, "it is what it is." What a lame way to avoid taking any responsibility for something that happens, even if you are the perpetrator.

My mother was all of 4ft. 9 in. tall, but if I had ever come home with a report card sporting D's and F's and responded to her questioning me as to why by informing her, "Well mom, it is what it is" I would likely still be unable to sit even today. More and more it seems that we use this phrase to excuse ourselves for not taking the time and effort to do things properly. We apply it to ourselves and to others. Recently we received a thank you card for a wedding gift we had given over two years ago. I was told it was OK, after all it "is what it is." I often do the cooking at home, and once burned the steaks to a cinder. I tried the old "it is what it is" on my wife, and she promptly straightened me out that it was "what I had made it." And that's the truth. Things are the way they are because we allow them to be that way.

Suppose God had looked down on us and instead of sending his Son had just said, "Oh well, it is what it is." This Lenten season let's make things what they should be and give up the shorthand phrases. God took accountability for us. We need to do the same in our own lives.

And now if you'll excuse me, I need to find help getting my groceries out to the car. It is what it is!

Wherein Dan's position in the pecking order of life is made perfectly clear

There we were, my wife Pat, our little dog Darby, and me, sitting peacefully on a bench outside of a small store on King Street in Alexandria, Virginia this past Saturday. We had come for the St. Patrick's Day Parade and the annual Fun Dog Show. We were all (and I do mean all) dressed in our Irish finery. As we were sitting there, a young woman stopped, said something about "looking so cute", and asked if she could take a picture. Of course we said yes. And so, I sucked in my stomach to accentuate my six pack abs (which over the years had morphed into more of a keg shape), smiled and waited for the flash. Pointing to me, the young woman said, "Could you slide over just a bit, you're blocking the puppy." I shifted over and heaved a heavy sigh causing the belt I was wearing to strain mightily in a futile effort to contain the aforementioned keg. This happened over and over again.

You would think at my age that ego would not be an issue, but we all like to think we are still attractive and worthy of an occasional photograph or two. It's true, Darby was by far the cutest of the three of us, and he had, after all, just won first place in the dog show for the best Irish outfit, but hey, I was important too, wasn't I. I was tempted to remind the young lady who had asked me to move that I wasn't, as the time honored phrase points out "chopped liver".

We humans have a tendency to see ourselves as always in competition with someone or some thing. Even as children we often find ourselves competing for the attention of our parents. In our work lives we may feel as if we are in competition with our fellow workers for recognition or promotion

In a world that encourages our competitive nature, isn't it comforting to know that with God, we are all favored? God's love isn't greater for me than it is for you or anyone else. We can't earn a greater place in His sight by what we wear or even what we do. He loves us, each one, despite our shortcomings. Even with a shape that no longer allows my body to be called a "temple", He loves me none the less. God will never ask any of us to "move over" for anyone else. We all have a place at His table.

And now, if you'll excuse me, I have to return a call from GQ Magazine, they want to do a feature spread on Darby.

Dan is told to "Go fly a kite!"

It seems as if the unseasonably warm weather, and the apparent early arrival of spring brings out the hidden child in some of us. On Saturday evening my lovely wife looked at me and said "You should go fly a kite." I didn't react. After all, that wasn't the first time I had received such a suggestion from her, and it was, in fact, a bit gentler than some others that I could recall. I went back to studying the finer details of the remote control in my hand, but she hadn't quite finished. "What's more," she said, "we should probably take a picnic lunch."

I saw an outdoor excursion shaping up, something I am not known for encouraging. After all, we humans have spent thousands of years creating climate controlled dwellings, and I rarely see any need to abandon them for the great outdoors. But I soon learned that a woman with a picnic basket cannot be ignored. And so, early Sunday afternoon we found ourselves (now the owners of top of the line $3.00 kites) making our way to Laurel Springs Regional Park in search of wind.

Within a little more than an hour we had accomplished all of the major segments of the kite flying experience. We had incorrectly assembled the kite then reassembled it; we had dashed madly across the empty field in an effort to get the kite airborne; we had yelled with joy when we experienced the exhilaration of a full 90 seconds of "flight" (why did my kite have to have Barbie and Ken on it?); we had lost control of one kite which went sailing off into the distance only to land on the other side of a chain-link fence; and we, of course, spent 15 minutes untangling the kite string from said chain-link fence.

It's all about the wind, isn't it?

Sometimes lifting our spirits which may be low because of personal or financial issues can seem a bit like trying to fly a kite. A lot of trial and error, and many false starts. Finding the right wind to lift a kite can be elusive, but in our personal lives we know that God is the "wind beneath our wings" and that with His help we can in fact soar like the eagles. And we don't need to wait for any particular weather pattern as His support is always available to us.

And now, if you'll excuse me, I need to digress just a bit. I was in the middle of writing this, when my granddaughter, Emma Grace, decided to make her world premiere. We dashed up to Baltimore to be there with my daughter Jennifer and her husband George for the grand event. God indeed lifts our spirits in many ways, but none more gratifying than seeing a new life enter into this world. Emma Grace is beautiful, God is good and we are all blessed. Be thankful each day for all that God gives to each of us.

Resisting Temptation

Temptation is a terrible thing. We are told by Jesus to resist it at all costs. Yet it is not easy. I say this as I sit at my desk in the church office looking hungrily at a box of donuts with somebody else's name on it. What is truly amazing is the amount of stress resisting this kind of temptation can generate. It's interesting that I have no problem resisting the temptation to take a wallet, a purse, or some other seriously valuable item that might be left in the office - but donuts! That's just a bit unfair, don't you think?

But I suppose that's the nature of temptation. It comes in all sorts of different packages and under many varied identities. Sometimes we see it as a message in our e-mail box offering us a way to get rich quick through a friendly Nigerian millionaire who was kind enough to name us in his will. Sometimes we might see it as an unexpected check that comes to us in an official looking envelope and advises us to cash it as soon as possible (did you notice the fine print that lets you know you've agreed to a high interest loan by cashing the check?) Sometimes it may even come from a friend urging us to do something that we know is not right because no one will ever find out.

We often approach temptation with the thought that we are strong enough to get close to it, just to investigate, without actually succumbing to its power. And so I sit here gazing across the slim barrier between my chair and that box of calories with its sweet smell wafting its way to my highly sensitive (but pleasantly shaped) nose. "I can just look," I say to myself. "That wouldn't hurt anything, right?" But there's a problem. The box is neatly wrapped with some ribbon tied in a pretty bow. How to do it? How to sneak a peek without leaving the tell-tale sign of an amateurishly tied bow? We are incredibly clever beings when it comes to finding ways to get what we want, and after much planning, I managed to ease the bow off of the box without actually untying it. I was just about to feast (my eyes that is) on those delectable morsels, when that intrusive telephone had the audacity to ring. It was a wrong number, but then I thought, perhaps it was a sign from above, a reminder that I had no business coveting my neighbor's cupcakes. Gingerly, I replaced the bow. Temptation avoided. And no one will ever know. After all, what are the chances of anyone actually reading this?

And now, if you'll excuse me, I hear a jelly donut calling my name

A rose by any other name might be pastrami

Ah Spring. The lilting tones of song birds perched on flowering trees float harmoniously in the air; the sweet fragrance of abundant flora dances magically around the nose. A light spring breeze carries it all on gentle wings. And I think, "What a glorious gift is our sense of smell."

I threw open the windows of the church office to bask in the sights sounds and smells of the gorgeous spring day. And I think, "An ice cold soda would surely enhance this wonderful experience." And so I go to the small refrigerator in the office and boldly and completely without fear open wide the door to beverage utopia.

Ah Spring! The warmth of the room caused me to recoil in olfactory horror as the pungent odor of 8 day old pastrami stored precariously in a half-sealed, bargain brand, plastic sandwich bag flew out of the dark recesses of the tiny fridge, and wiped out any remnants of the scented bliss of spring flowers. And I think, "Why did God give us noses?"

But maybe there was a higher purpose to that decaying lunch meat then just offending my sensitive nature. Perhaps I was meant to discover it. Perhaps the staleness of the air within the fridge was meant to contrast with the freshness of the air outside of the office. Spring is, after all, a time when the staleness of winter gives way to new growth and God lifts His broom, and sweeps clean His beautiful landscapes.

Easter is just a week away, and as we celebrate the resurrection of our Lord and the new life promised to all of us, perhaps we should see it as a time of renewal in our own lives. Perhaps we should consider this the perfect opportunity to inventory our habits and behaviors; to look deep within the back recesses of our personalities; to root out those things that are no longer useful to us.

Most of us work hard to keep the clutter out of our refrigerators. Perhaps it's wise to do the same for our thinking and our behavior.

And now, if you'll excuse me, I need to speak to someone about a pastrami sandwich.

Does God Shop at Wal-Mart?
Small Miracle in a Big Box Store

Alright, alright, I know already. I know God isn't burdened with the mundane task of grocery shopping. And during the Easter season, I'm almost positive He isn't out shopping for goodies to fill waiting Easter baskets. And even if He were, it's more likely He'd be a Whole Foods kind of shopper rather than searching out bargains at Wal-Mart.

But the simple fact is I think God did visit the Wal-Mart in La Plata this past weekend - and I think He was there for me. What irrefutable proof do I have of this visitation? An Easter Egg. But not just any Easter egg. A genuine, original, undamaged, rare, and highly sought-after Mary Sue Vanilla Butter Cream Egg.

Despite encouraging words from some of my friends here at Peace (you can call off your search now), I had pretty much resigned myself to a year without a VBCE (vanilla butter cream egg). And so I was not prepared for my surprise. My wife and I had just returned from spending Easter day with our new granddaughter, and I wandered over to the Easter basket my wife had setup the night before. As I rummaged despondently through the usual assortment of chocolate bunnies, edible carrots, plastic bouncing chickens and colorful Peeps, I saw it. As Captain Ahab once said while looking for Moby Dick, "There he lay!" Beautifully boxed, sitting on a bed of green grass and ripe for the picking, was a Mary Sue Vanilla Butter Cream Egg!

I found myself stammering in disbelief to my wife, "How? Where? Why? Who."

"I can't explain it." she said, "I walked into Wal-Mart and there it was, the last one!"

"But, we were just in there," I reminded her, "and there was nothing!"

"I know. It's a small miracle." she replied.

God is like that, isn't He? Just when you think your prayers will never be answered; when you've given up and lost hope; He is there, right on time. The gospel music group of which I am a part ("Joyful Noise") sings a song called "On Time God." The lyrics include these lines:

> "He's an on-time God, yes he is"
> "He may not come when you want Him,
>   but He'll be there right on time."

Now I don't pretend to think that God made my desire for a VBCE a priority, but I do believe that He hears our prayers, and knows our needs, and that if we just trust in Him, we will receive not only what we need, but even sometimes those things that we do not. God loves you, and He loves me enough to grant even my most unnecessary desire.

And now if you'll excuse me, I've got a VBCE to enjoy, and a prayer of thanks to deliver to a generous and loving God.

Too Much Love...Or, Is That Really Your Desktop Background?

According to one definition, a purist is "one who desires that an item remain true to its essence and free from adulterating or diluting influences." Most people who know me would say that describes my behavior in a lot of areas. It's particularly true when it comes to my computer. Some people love to decorate their monitors or laptops with stickers, or other personal touches, and many people take advantage of the fact that you can change the "desktop background" on your monitor to anything you might like. Not me. I'm a Windows person through and through, and I have always believed that if Bill Gates had wanted me to have a picture of a waterfall on my screen, he would have put one there. I saw the flowing windows flag logo as a thing of beauty, a force of nature not to be lightly shoved aside.

My best friend has for years replaced his desktop background with photos of his grandchildren. They are beautiful children to be sure, but locating an icon on the desktop of his computer is almost impossible. I once tried to start Microsoft Word by clicking repeatedly on what turned out to be a 2 year old's nose.

This was the "dark side" of computing to me. And so, it was with some surprise that I one day found myself, while looking at pictures of my new granddaughter, Emma Grace, muttering that she might look good as a desktop background. And suddenly my mouse took on the characteristics of a Ouija board "planchette" (the little device you rest your fingers on), and without conscious effort, my iconic Windows desktop was gone, and there was Emma Grace gazing back at me in all her glory.

I was sure that I heard Bill Gates crying as another purist left the fold. The slippery slope of personalization had embraced me, and before I knew it I had become the Grandpa that Internet retailers dream of.

I saw Emma's face on everything, cups, mugs, t-shirts, and tote bags. And that was just on the first site I visited. As I clicked the button to order my photo stamps, I started to wonder, was this insanity, had I gone too far? I thought of stopping, but then I realized, why? Why should I stop? Could there ever be such a thing as too much love? She was beautiful, and I wanted to see her wherever I looked.

So too, does God find each one of us beautiful. And if He has a computer I imagine a desktop overflowing with ICONS for each one of His children. God's love for us is boundless. Perhaps being a purist means embracing the idea that there can never be too much love.

And now if you'll excuse me, my best friend is on his way over, and I've got to turn off my computer before he discovers I've gone over to the "dark side". But, you know what? It's delightful over there.

Spending Mother's Day in the Bathroom

I will be thinking of my mom today. And I will be doing it in the bathroom. She left this earth about 2 ½ years ago at the age of 95. She had spent the last 3 years of her life living with my wife and me. It was a time of great challenge for us, but also one that allowed us to be close to her during her declining years. There are many things I miss about my mom, her sense of humor (some say she passed it on to me), her generosity, and one that seems especially relevant, as Mother's Day approaches, was her commitment to the memory of family and friends who had departed.

She never missed an opportunity to place flowers on the altar on birthdays and anniversaries. She made sure we always kept fresh arrangements on my dad's grave. She would remind us of birthdays long after the celebrant had passed, and seemed genuinely disappointed that she could not send a gift. She tried to be very businesslike about it, but her sentimentality was obvious to all.

So how to honor her memory when she passed was a question we pondered very seriously. Mom loved church. She went with us every Sunday, and she also participated in a seniors group at her former church. Everyone knew her as "Mom". What a tribute that was in itself, knowing that so many people thought of her in that way. My wife and I were draining our creative juices, but no clear idea of how to remember her was crystallizing for us.

But God provides. One Sunday we heard the news that the church was looking to add 3 additional stained glass windows. We knew immediately that a memorial window would be a wonderful tribute to my mom. When I spoke to the coordinator of the project he offered to show us the 3 options. The windows were to be on either side of the church's original main entrance. Although not used anymore, this was the side of the church facing the main road. The first location turned out to be in what had been turned into a closet. The second was actually a transom over the old main entrance. Neither of those locations appealed to us. Our third and final option turned out to be in a room just outside of the Sanctuary and off the Narthex. It was a heavily used room which held a special place in my 95 year old mom's heart. It was the first place she wanted to go after every service. It was the bathroom.

At first we thought, no, this wouldn't be right or seemly. But then we remembered two things; my mom's incredible sense of humor, and the number of trips she had made to that room in her last years. I could hear her laughing at the thought of so many people seeing her memorial in a place where they could take their time looking at it. And we laughed too. It was appropriate.

The window is absolutely beautiful, and at night when the lights inside are on, it is visually stunning from the road.

And so this Sunday, today, I will be remembering my mom in many different ways, and I'll be starting with a visit to "her" room. Thank God for moms young and old, and for the memories and the smiles they give us.

And now, if you'll excuse me, I'm heading to the bathroom for a good laugh with my mom.

Making Music - It's the Human Thing to Do.

We are born with certain natural tendencies, things that we just seem to know how to do. It's called instinct. We know how to breathe, we know how to eat, and, as I was recently reminded by a new grandbaby, we know how to poop (can I say "poop" in a church bulletin?) OK, so maybe those aren't skills with the potential to move humanity to the next plateau, but there is another skill that seems to come naturally to us humans that just might - making music.

I noticed this phenomena on display this past weekend as my wife and I were babysitting for our granddaughter, Emma Grace, so that her first-time mom and dad could enjoy a quiet Mother's Day dinner alone. We'd been shown several devices that were "guaranteed" to soothe little Emma should she show her displeasure with our grandparenting skills. One device reminded me of Edgar Allen Poe's iconic short story "The Pit and the Pendulum." It was a large contraption that you placed the baby into (the pit) and then pressed a button which began an endless pendulum-like motion designed to rock the restless child into submission (while watching it, I think I ended up hypnotized and clucking like a hen.) But the most impressive device was a mat on which Emma could lie. Over her head dangled numerous playful animals, and at the foot of the mat there was a soft piano keyboard that played musical notes and tunes when activated by the baby's kick. Needless to say, *OUR* granddaughter exhibited an instant mastery of rhythm and tempo, and we saw a Julliard scholarship only a few short years away.

The wonderful thing about music is that you don't have to be particularly good at it to enjoy its benefits. As a child I was "forced" to play a diabolical instrument called a fluteophone. I struggled to learn such complex pieces as "Twinkle, Twinkle, Little Star", and "Row, Row, Row Your Boat" (I'm darn close to getting both of them.) In the 3rd grade, while trying out for my elementary school glee club, I was advised to take up painting. My parents were well ahead of their time when they told me that should a TV show ever be developed in which amateur singers compete to become rock stars, I should call in sick to the auditions.

Still, I love music, and it's an important part of my current life. I've gotten a little better at some things, and the benefits are fantastic. Good, bad, or somewhere in between, music is for everyone. Our Little Emma Grace will be encouraged to start early and practice often.

Our prayer life is very much like music. It doesn't matter how proficient we are at praying. All that matters is that we practice it frequently. And as with music, the benefits are there for us regardless of our proficiency. We will encourage Emma Grace in this as well.

And now if you'll excuse me, there's a fluteophone begging to be dusted off and abused.

Render unto Caesar that which is Caesar's or, A Tale of Two Salads

It is often said that good things come in small packages. While that is true for jewelry and other valuable trinkets, it does not hold true for micro fridges.

Returning to the church office on Mondays can often be a bit of a challenge. The office is used for a lot of different things over the course of a weekend, and frequently becomes a storage site for miscellaneous objects, but the little micro-fridge sitting lonely and unobserved in a corner of the room often gets the unkindest gifts of all. They are gifts that keep on giving.

Such was the case this past Monday when two pathetic looking plastic containers found their way onto the top shelf of the fridge. In what I concluded was a somewhat confused attempt to follow the teachings of Jesus, the owner (he who shall not be named) rendered unto each one a generous portion of Caesar salad dressing. The plastic containers were woefully inadequate at retaining the essence of the dressing which had permeated the other contents of the little ice box.

While slathering a generous portion of cream cheese onto my Monday morning bagel, I was greeted by the malodorous scent of garlic and vinegar which seemed to have infused itself into the very heart of Philadelphia's finest creation. Even the poppy seeds on my bagel couldn't overcome the power of the great Caesar (salad, that is).

Suddenly I found myself bemoaning the death of the clothespin. Surely, that little device could have pinched off the offensive odor.

The message came through loud and clear: "I love salads and I want everyone to know it!" Or, I wondered, was the message really "Hey, you're eating too many bagels. Stop!"

Sometimes we all have the tendency to want to shout our feelings and beliefs to the world. We want people to know us; who we are and what's important to us. And so we wear t-shirts with messages, sport bumper stickers or vanity license plates on our cars, or proclaim vocally that our way is the right way (think politicians.)

As Christians we are called to follow the teachings of Jesus, but to do so humbly and with a servant's heart. We do not need to shout our faith, it's enough to live as Christ lived, and share His love with the world.

And now if you'll excuse me, there are two nondescript containers of what may be soup sitting ominously on the top shelf of the fridge.

Who Am I?

Dr. Seuss had a way with words. In his masterpiece, "Green Eggs and Ham", he opens with the main character uttering this memorable line, "I am Sam." Then as if to be sure we heard it correctly, he reminds us, "I am Sam." And finally, just to drive the point home he announces, "Sam I Am." This was someone who clearly knew just exactly who he was.

Apparently that's something many of us can't say. Back in the day (eons ago) we used to declare that we couldn't do anything productive because we had to "find ourselves". That often meant wandering around in a cloud for several years using up our parents' money while attempting to locate our missing personalities. I never have found myself. I do vaguely remember seeing me in a comic book store in 1962, and once in 1965 buying a used 8 Track tape player at a yard sale.

I once tried to convince my wife that I would be a much better husband if she would just understand that I needed to go out on Friday nights to "find myself." She told me not to bother as she knew exactly where I could find myself - in the bathroom fixing the toilet as she had asked me to do 9 times.

Times have changed. Apparently everyone has now indeed found themselves, and the new rallying cry is "I just want people to know who I am." I was watching a competition to determine the next Food Network Star, and at least 3 of the contestants' mentors kept insisting that their charges needed to show people "who they were." And 70% of the contestants acknowledged that they hadn't done that, but they were determined (they often said this in tears) to make sure that in the next round we would know "who they were." I watched the show twice and I still don't have any idea who these folks were, are, or may be in the future.

I'm not sure which is more frustrating, people looking for themselves, or people insisting that you have to get to know them now that they have found themselves.

Do we ever really know who we are? Do we ever really know who anyone else is? How often have you heard neighbors reporting, "He was always a quiet, gentle person" right after someone commits a terrible crime? There is only one who really knows us. One who knows what's truly in our hearts. If we really want to find ourselves, we need to ask God to give us the answer. And if we want people to know who we truly are, then we need to follow the advice that God gives us through prayer. The answer won't be found by w0ndering and it can't be learned in a cooking competition. God knows who we are, and he wants us to know too.

And now, if you'll excuse me, I have to hook up my 8 Track player so I'll have some music while fixing the toilet.

Babbling as an Art Form

Babies babble. I don't suppose that comes as a startling revelation to anyone who's ever been around an infant. We had a wonderful Memorial Day visit from our granddaughter Emma Grace, who demonstrated that she had more than mastered the fine art of babbling.

But did you know that babbling is not limited to those still in diapers? I know this because I have been accused from time to time of doing just that - babbling. Just the other day I was explaining to my sainted wife the inner workings of her cell phone when she turned to me and said, "What are you babbling about?" Never one to miss an opportunity to turn the tables, I made the same observation as she was verbalizing a list of things I needed to do while she was out.

To be honest, I'm an inveterate babbler. I do it while watching the nightly news. I do it behind the wheel when challenged by other drivers. I do it while standing in lines for any reason (but especially those where the major holdup is deciding how many extra pickles are really needed on that Quarter Pounder.) I babble when paying bills. I babble loudly when I can't locate the remote control. In short, I babble at life.

So what exactly is babbling? Well, here are a few definitions:

1. To utter a meaningless confusion of words or sounds
2. To make a continuous low, murmuring sound, as flowing water.
3. Inarticulate or meaningless talk or sounds.
4. To talk foolishly or idly; chatter

Oops, sorry, those were definitions of "Congress." But close enough.

God punished the builders of the Tower of Babel for their vanity in trying to build a stairway to heaven by causing them to speak different languages, making it impossible for them to communicate with each other. And it seems we've been babbling ever since.

We teach babies to speak intelligibly yet we often confound each other with confusing, meaningless, or foolish talk. We say what we want sometimes without thinking of the consequences or effects on others. But when we converse with God - when we pray - He can sort out the truth and honesty from behind the protective screen of our babbling. We should talk to each other just as we would to God.

And now, if you'll excuse me, I'm going to go babble to my granddaughter, she will not judge me. She'll just enjoy the conversation.

Through the Rear View Mirror

As I was driving to church last Sunday I stopped to allow a gray haired couple to cross the street. They were holding hands, dressed very neatly, and obviously heading for the church that was just in front of them. As I glanced at the couple in my rear view mirror, I said something to myself along the lines of, "No jeans for those folks; the older generation still knows how to dress for church." Catching my own reflection in the mirror I gasped, "Wait, I AM the older generation."

It was a rude and uncalled for reminder that I'm getting older. The wonderful thing about aging, is that most of the time, we don't realize it's happening to us. The other guy, sure, but not us. We're just the same as we were 20, 30 or more years ago. As I'm driving, I often look over at other cars poking along in the fast lane and mumble things like "That guy's so old he ought to be driving a walker, not a car." I'm so busy critiquing the other guy that I rarely notice the people in cars passing me who might well be making the same observation about my driving.

In grocery stores I never know whether to be happy or annoyed when a young bagger looks at me and asks if I need help carrying my container of Ovaltine out to my car. OK, I do happily accept the senior discount at the movie theater, and the free "senior" soda at Popeyes, but would it hurt them once in a while to ask to see some identification before automatically providing the discount. Once in a while, if I'm asked "Would you like the senior discount?" I stumble and say. "Sure, I'd like it, but I'm just a bit too young." They give it to me anyway.

If it wasn't that my waist size keeps expanding, and my joints sound a bit like tuning an old violin, I might delude myself into thinking I was still 30. But you know what, at the end of the day, I don't think I would like to go back and do things again. Each stage in my life has offered different challenges and rewards - some good, some not so good, but all memorable. Why go back and repeat what I have already known when it's so much more fun to keep moving forward to new and surprising experiences? God doesn't ask us to go back and change who we were yesterday, but he does want us to change who we are today and who we will be tomorrow. It isn't a matter of age, it's a matter of attitude.

And now, if you'll excuse me, I've got to get out to my car. The kid from the grocery store wants to know where to put the Metamucil.

Beware the Allure of an Oasis

There I was, it was early, maybe 7am, enjoying the rare experience of being the only one in the express checkout lane of a local supermarket. I surveyed my surroundings much as Edmund Hillary must have done on reaching the summit of Mt. Everest. If I'd had a flag I would have planted it squarely in the middle of the plastic bag holder. Confidently I "swiped" my store courtesy card through the card reader - "Card Read Error", the machine flashed back at me. Defiantly I swiped the card again. "Card Read Error" the little machine insisted. Again and again I pushed, pulled, and shoved the worn bit of plastic through the sadistic jaws of the card reader only to be rebuffed again and again. And now there were two other people in line to whom I had deprived the small victory of a quick checkout.

Finally surrendering, I handed the card to the clerk. Once more I had been beaten by technology. As I picked up my bag to leave, there, gleaming in the reflected early morning sunlight was a sign with the magical words

"Customer Service." It stood like an oasis in the quiet desert that was the supermarket. There was no one in line. "Two victories in one day", I thought to myself. I approached cautiously, but was greeted by a smiling young woman, who spoke words of comfort to me, "How can I help you Sir?"

"It's my store card," I told her, as if reporting a bad day at school to my mother, "it won't work right."

"Did you try entering your phone number?" She said to me with a tone that was not quite motherly.

"Yes, yes, I did, but it came up with the name Mildred Morgenstein. I'm not Mildred Morgenstein."

"Sounds like your card is not working right sir." she observed with the keen perception that can only come from months of intensive customer service training.

"Yes," I said, "but you can help me right?"

"Of course, sir," she said "at this store, we're all about customer service."

Sensing success within my grasp, I said, "Great, I'd like a new card."

"Oh, we can't do that here." she said. "Huh?" I replied as I felt the oasis dry up and blow away leaving me thirsty and alone.

And now, if you'll excuse me there's a call from me I have to take. It's from a Mildred Morgenstein.

My New Best Friends

I'd like to introduce you to Pedro and Rowena, my new best friends. Actually, they are my Sirius/XM Listener Care representatives. And they are committed to my listening satisfaction. I know this because they tell me so at the end of every conversation.

In case you're still tuning in to your music on that old Philco console in your living room, Sirius/XM is a pay satellite radio system that operates in much the same way as cable or satellite TV. Many newer cars are equipped to receive the signals, and you can buy portable receivers for use in home or elsewhere. The allure is that you can receive 140+ stations virtually anywhere in the country without worrying about losing the signal as the car travels. A secondary incentive is the promise of commercial-free music stations. Of course, folks younger than 40 will tell you that even this is somewhat outdated thanks to services like Pandora which offer free radio through your iPhone or other device. But Pandora doesn't have Pedro and Rowena.

Pedro and Rowena have become my "chat" buddies. Now to be fair, I suspect that these may not be their real names, and that they change them frequently. I envision anonymous people answering calls in some country whose name has more consonants than vowels and picking a name to use for each call from a list on the desk in front of them. Still, I like Rowena because the name conjures up visions of the beautiful Saxon heroine from Sir Walter Scott's "Ivanhoe", a book I've always loved.

But Rowena doesn't love me. Neither she nor Pedro have been able to resolve my issue with subscribing to XM radio. We chat daily. I calmly explain my problem, and my chat buddy calmly types in the boilerplate answer from the company script. Each chat session becomes progressively less calm for me, but Rowena never falters, always remaining calm, apologetic, and determined to give me the same answer which manages to avoid the central issue in my question. I've even tried rewording the question, but the lovely Rowena is unflappable as she hits F6 on her keyboard to insert the required response.

Rowena and Pedro are not good listeners. God is. When we pray to him we can be sure he is going to understand us, and that his response will be tailored to us. God doesn't have an agenda. He's not trying to sell us anything. He just wants us to be happy and to love him as he loves each of us.

And we don't need expensive subscriptions or special equipment to stay in communication with God. He's available 24 hours a day 7 days a week. All we have to do is ask for him.

And now if you'll excuse me, I've got work to do. Rowena and Pedro are coming over. We're going to have a barbecue and a nice chat on how they can assure my continued listening satisfaction with XM Radio.

Toto - I have a feeling we're not in Kansas anymore

Maybe it's because I'm in rehearsals for "The Wizard of Oz" at the Port Tobacco Theater (warning, shameless self-promotion season is once again upon us), or perhaps it was just the shock of stepping outdoors into temperatures that went beyond the limits of the ancient temperature sensing devices in my car, but either way, I was firmly convinced I was no longer in the "Land of Pleasant Living" as National Bohemian Beer once called this area (can you say, "I'm old enough to remember Nat Bo"?)

Between the heat, humidity and the storms we experienced during the last week of June, our patience and resourcefulness were tested to their limits. Because I hadn't bothered to restock a certain large size battery, I was reduced to using the light from my cell phone camera to stumble around the house looking for that elusive box of matches so that I could light the few candle stubs that remained after the last blackout. In fact my cell phone's fragile 3G network proved to be our only workable contact with the outside world. FIOS was down which meant no Internet, limited phone capability, and no reruns of CSI. Even the radio station I was able to tune via my phone mocked me by suggesting everyone should turn on their battery powered devices to stay in touch - except for that guy in La Plata who didn't bother to stock up on batteries.

My wife Pat and I decided, what the heck, let's just play some board games by candlelight, it would be fun. Then we realized our board games were all electronic. The Wii wouldn't work, and even our ancient copy of "Operation" needed, you guessed it, batteries. So we moved to cards, but our battery operated card shuffler was dead (did people really do that by hand in the day?). We tried that old party favorite "Twister", but we couldn't see the colors in the dark. It was shaping up to be a long night. We thought about just going to bed, but the white noise machine that masked my snoring wasn't working and Pat's constant elbowing me in the side would just keep me awake as well. Desperate for entertainment, I yanked my View Master Model G (kids, ask your parents) out of the mothball covered box in the basement, and we took turns looking at discs of the Grand Canyon. It was a long night.

The weather is unpredictable, despite the pitiful efforts of highly paid meteorologists to do so. Last week's storm arrived with virtually no warning. Our efforts to deal with forces greater then ourselves usually end in dismal failure. In times of crisis we turn to God for help, the one constant in an ever changing environment. And he is there for us, to guide us and to point us to the right path. I wonder if perhaps we shouldn't consider turning to God for that same guidance in our daily lives. He knows the path through the darkness, and he can guide us through the daylight as well.

And now, if you'll excuse me, I need to finish signing up for the Battery of the Month Club.

It Isn't Easy Being Green

According to Kermit the Frog, it isn't easy being green. I generally don't look to frogs for life lessons, but having just completed the final week of intensive rehearsals for "The Wizard of Oz" (did I mention it opened Friday with a matinée today?) I am coming around to his way of thinking.

I have two roles in this production; the venerable Uncle Henry, and the Guard of Oz. (you know, the "HA HA HA, HO HO HO...Merry Old Land of Oz guy). Now Uncle Henry's pretty straight forward. He looks like your typical mid-western farmer. But the Guard? Well, that's a horse of a different color - green to be exact.

The wonderful costumers at PTP (led this time by my wife Pat) have designed a form fitting outfit that takes green to new levels. The costume is spectacular (not so much the form in it.) Topped off by oversized eyebrows and a handlebar mustache I am quite the sight to behold.

Of course there are a few challenges that come with looking so good. I can't bend over to touch my toes (OK, so I really couldn't do that before either), I can't breathe very well through the thick mustache, and the whole thing gets pretty hot after a while. Still, the goal is to make an impression, and when I step through the gates of Emerald City, I think I will do just that.

In fact, all of the costumes in this production are spectacular. The Munchkins are, of course, adorable. The Scarecrow, Tin Man and Lion are just what you would expect. There are some surprises - I don't think you will ever see apple trees quite like those in this production, and the Jitterbugs, well, you'll just have to see them to believe them.

It's fun to dress up, whether for a theatrical production, Halloween, or just for the fun of it. We do it as children very naturally, and as adults, well, we still do it, but we hide behind Renaissance Fairs or other "excuses." Sometimes we dress up to impress people, and sometimes perhaps just to shock them. Some of us may even think that the way we dress defines "who we are." We may think that by dressing a certain way we can disguise our flaws or enhance how others perceive us.

God doesn't worry much about how we dress. He knows and understands what's in our hearts. He wants us to be happy with the way He made us. To God we are beautiful just the way we are.

As Kermit sings in the last line of "It Isn't Easy Being Green":

> *It could make you wonder why, but why wonder why? Wonder, I am green and it'll do fine, it's beautiful! And I think it's what I want to be.*

And now, if you'll excuse me I've got a mustache to style.

Prayer in Unexpected Places

Christians and regular church goers are generally not surprised to encounter people praying. They're used to seeing families or couples saying grace before a meal in a restaurant, and thanks to men like Tim Tebow they have even grown accustomed to sports figures expressing their faith publicly. But sometimes prayer can show up in unexpected places.

Back in the day (William Shakespeare's day to be exact) actors were not held in very high regard. In fact, acting was considered such a dishonorable profession that women were simply not permitted to participate. All roles were played by men or boys. Fortunately that attitude has changed somewhat, and while there are, no doubt, dishonorable actors, performing on the stage is now regarded much more favorably.

Still, our image of actors and actresses doesn't always conjure up images of prayer sessions. But then, you haven't been backstage at the Port Tobacco Theater, where prayer is much more common than you might think.

The current production of "The Wizard of Oz" is a good example. The cast for this show is some 50+ people with better than half being made up of children (Munchkins, you know.) Would it surprise you to hear that every single performance is preceded by a large prayer circle backstage? That's right, and what's even more remarkable is that the organizers of the prayer are often teenagers and children. With both adults and kids holding hands, prayers are offered for the success of the show, thanks given for the talents that God has provided to the cast, and healing asked for those who may be in need that evening.

Would it also surprise you to know that many of the younger children in the cast are often the most vocal during the prayers? It is incredibly inspirational to hear those children speaking so honestly and easily about their faith.

No one is forced to participate, and not everyone does, but there is a naturalness about the process that is hard to describe. During last year's production of "A Christmas Carol" one of the cast members suffered a heart attack. He received prayers before every performance asking that he be healed and allowed to return to the show. He was and he did.

I don't know if prayers will make me a better performer, but I do know that the prayer circle at the theater has allowed me to be in the company of some wonderful young people. With children like these we need have no fear for the future. It is in good hands.

And now, if you'll excuse me, I need to prepare for another performance this afternoon, and another opportunity to pray with some wonderful people.

Where's a Man to Go?

There was a time when a man could escape for a few blissful moments. Escape from the hustle and bustle of daily life, the din of playful children, and the always present honey-do list. Escape to a place where a man could be a man. A place women never entered. A place rife with the smell of tobacco, protected by layers of untouched dust, with piles of unswept hair clippings dotted like mini islands on a black and white linoleum floor. A place where mustached men wielded straight razors and scissors and knew how to use them. A place where sports and politics were tossed about like unpinned hand grenades, and where talk of relationships meant a man and his car. No, my friends, it wasn't heaven, just the local Barbershop.

But no more, that day is gone, replaced by frou-frou shops that want to wash your hair, manicure your nails, touch up your eye brows, and add just a hint of color to your graying hair. Walking in to one of the ubiquitous unisex hair salons that dot the landscape these days is akin to stumbling into a baby shower without a "onesie" to your name. Out of place and out of time is the way I feel as I'm escorted to the hair washing station to have them do the same thing I did just an hour earlier at home. And as I'm lying back with my head in a very unnatural position, I imagine the "stylists" exchanging comments about my mismatched socks, or unkempt shirt.

Conversation is difficult because I have no idea what happened on "Bachelorette" the night before, and I didn't know Oprah had moved to her own channel.

Now to be clear, the folks working in these salons are talented and know what they are doing. Still, I have never had the nerve to ask for a shave - my legs are fine just the way they are.

Men come in, women come in, men with children come in, and women with children come in. Every possible combination and age group is represented. Natural male tendencies to scratch in certain places are greatly inhibited. I need to be on my best behavior. I leave smelling of lilacs and roses and in desperate need of a good pat down with Clubman Talcum Powder.

My experience with hair grooming included the traditional "bowl" treatment by my mother when money was tight, but I eventually moved on to the world of "real" haircuts at the local barbershop. I just don't know if I can make this last leap to the unisex salon.

Technology and progress are wonderful, but sometimes there is no substitute for the traditional. Barbers used to know how to cut men's hair. Sure they used electric trimmers now and again, but mostly for quick touch ups. The real skill was in using those small scissors to give a precise cut. Now, the stylist plugs in one of those mini lawn mowers, runs it over your scalp, and calls it a day.

Society is moving away from the traditional in a constant race to do things more quickly and easily. The idea of putting any effort or thought into what we do is no longer considered worthwhile.

That works for some things, but not all. Sure, we can read Bibles online, join in interactive chats about religion, add our names to electronic prayer lists, but none of those things can replace the experience of being in a real church with real people, sharing God's very real love.

And now, if you'll excuse me, I need to find a suitably shaped bowl for my wife to use when my next haircut is due.

Learning the Sign Language of McDonalds

Have you noticed? We live in an increasingly noisy world. Wherever we go, whatever we do, we are bombarded by misguided purveyors of sound who believe that louder is better. We turn on our televisions to relax, and find ourselves desperately trying to understand the dialog over the music and sound effects. Then come the commercials - amped up another 20 decibels. Our "fine dining" experiences are negated by background music designed more, it seems, for the pleasure of the staff than of the patrons. Rather than complementing and enhancing our meal, the booming rhythm and repetitive bass simply induce indigestion and headache. Try ordering a pate de foie gras appetizer in one of those places. I did and ended up with a patty melt for four.

Ever watch "Dancing with the Stars"? It's almost impossible to hear the announcers over the incessant clapping, cheering, and whistling that the audience is apparently required to engage in non-stop. At my age I don't think I could see the show live. I'd be exhausted by the first commercial break. Used to be you waited for something to actually happen before applauding. Now it seems there is a primal fear of any sort of silence.

Even McDonalds, never known for its quiet atmosphere, has upped its game. They've added these Frappe machines that grind ice at decibel levels rivaling the sound of a navy ice breaker struggling through the arctic ice flow. To even order a basic Quarter Pounder you are reduced to a form of sign language as you try to gesture and hold up fingers to indicate what order number you want. And you don't want to know what the hand signal is for "hold the onions".

I'm convinced the next big innovation in aftermarket car accessories will be total soundproofing to protect us from those drivers who are determined to torture others with their obnoxious and indecipherable heavy metal, rap, headbanger (substitute your personal favorite), "music". When your car's speaker system is larger than its engine, it may be time to reevaluate your priorities. One of my favorite reactions when stopped at a traffic light next to one of these socially inept drivers is to change my radio to the classical station, roll down my windows and match them decibel for decibel. It's fun to watch them squirm.

The world is noisy, and part of our problem as a society is that we can't communicate effectively in that kind of environment. We just can't hear each other. But just as a mother can hear the cries of her baby above any noise, so too can God hear each one of us clearly even through the babble of millions of voices speaking at once. God loves us enough to listen for each and every prayer. What a miracle in a noisy world.

And now, if you'll excuse me, I need to look up the hand signal for a large order of fries.

What's a guy have to do to shop in peace in quiet?

I'm a shopper. There, I've said it. I know, I know, my membership in the species male is in jeopardy of being revoked, but I can't help it. It's my mother's fault. She loved to shop, and I now think that for the first few years of our lives my brother and I were tethered to clothing racks in New Jersey department stores (I have the marks on my ankles to prove it.) My mom kept her love of shopping well into her 90s. But she was also responsible for giving me the yearning to shop alone.

You see, my mom was not a quiet person. A New Yorker by birth, she was prone to speaking very loudly in public situations. And as her hearing deteriorated the problem got ever worse. In grocery stores she would shout out with great gusto a never ending string of instructions to me. "Find the yellow mustard!" "Where's the milk?" "How much is that cereal?" "Don't forget my headache pills." Oh, I was pretty sure I wouldn't forget the headache pills (they'd be open before I got to the checkout stand.) I'd let her check out in aisle 1 while I went to the other end of the lanes in a vain attempt to gain some anonymity since my mother had the unpleasant habit of explaining all of her purchases to the amusement of the checkout clerk. "Oh," she would say, "these cookies aren't for me. My son just can't stop eating them, and The Beano is for my son, he has a bit of a gas problem."

I tried to ignore her, but she would inevitably spy me 10 lanes away and scream in her loudest voice "Danny, Danny, I found that Preparation H you were looking for - got you the large tube!. And don't forget to clean out the bathroom when you get home."

And so, I longed for the ability to shop alone without fear and in peace and quiet. My mom passed away a couple of years ago, and I miss her greatly. I even think I miss the times we spent in the grocery store.

But God provides. Not wanting to stand in long lines, I generally use the self-checkout lanes, where I am convinced my mother had part time work recording the incessant instructions screamed at you from those machines. "Scan your club card!" "Scan your first item!" "Move your item to the bagging area!" "Unexpected item in bagging area!" "Bagging area full!

Some of them even announce the item and price just as my mother would have done, loudly and for all the world to hear, "PREPARATION H, Large Tube, 3.99" "Move your PREPARATION H to the bagging area!"

I know it's weird, but every time I checkout from a grocery store, I remember those times with my mom. And I smile.

And now, if you'll excuse me, I have to get home and clean the bathroom.

Babies are just miniature women in onesies.

Being outsmarted (sometimes snookered) by a woman is nothing new for me. It happens almost every day. Women seem to have an innate ability to maneuver this unsuspecting male to do their bidding, and convince me that it was my idea at the same time.

When my granddaughter Emma Grace was born, I silently rejoiced that here, at last, would be a female I might have a chance at outsmarting. Unfortunately, I had forgotten this quote by May Sarton: "Don't forget that compared to a grownup person every baby is a genius."

It would be a mistake (I know because I've made it) to think that babies are limited to eating, sleeping, crying and other basic instincts. Their ability to manipulate grown-ups is quite sophisticated.

This past weekend while watching grandma and the new mom and dad holding Emma and trying vainly to figure out what she wanted that would ease the crying, I saw some signs of a very clever mind at work (not mom & dad's.)

Always observant, I don't think Emma realized that I was watching from a comfortable seat. Her tears and cries were cleverly directed towards the three unwary caregivers and were eliciting the desired response - attention. But, and I saw this multiple times, when she turned away from their gaze, I saw a twinkle in her eye and a wry smile that said "Now I've got them."

I wanted to say to my wife and daughter, "You know she's playing you, don't you?" But before I could do so, my wife handed little Emma to me and said "See what you can do." See what I can do? Are you kidding? So there I was, and all my brilliant observations couldn't save me. I found myself doing the same things the others had tried. As I laid her down and began to tickle her tummy (I never thought I'd be saying things like this), she formed the most perfect smile I had ever seen. And just that quickly it was over. Any thought of besting this little beauty in the brains department vanished. I was in her power.

James Matthew Barrie said to Wendy in his novel "Peter Pan", "...when the first baby laughed for the first time, the laugh broke into a thousand pieces and they all went skipping about, and that was the beginning of fairies."

There is nothing like a baby's smile and laughter to remind us that in God's universe, these little wonders are the masters of us all.

And now, if you'll excuse me, there's a tummy somewhere that needs to be rubbed.

The Secret War to End Haggling

My wife and I both like to browse through antique shops and flea markets. She's always looking for cruets to add to her mother's collection, old hats, dress forms or other items related to costuming and sewing. Me, I'm mostly looking for old corkscrews or other wine related paraphernalia (or, come to think of it, old wine.) Has anyone noticed that the "older" we get, the more we seem to be looking for "old" stuff?

Part of the fun and challenge of buying antiques is negotiating over the price. Now I'm not embarrassed to admit that I'm addicted to shows like "American Pickers", "Pawn Stars" and their many imitators, and so I understand that the price marked is not really the price you should pay. Dealers always price things higher than what they will accept, and buyers always offer less than they are willing to pay. Having said that, I acknowledge that I'm not always a particularly savvy negotiator.

But it's becoming harder and harder to bargain these days (maybe that's an unintended consequence of our never compromise political system.) A good case in point was a recent trip Pat and I took to Strasburg, Virginia. We were there to visit some Civil War sites, but the lure of an enormous building, The Strasburg Emporium, was like the call of the Sirens to us. The Emporium was one of those maze like affairs in which you continually think you are in the last room only to find 3 more branching out from behind dusty bookcases. As we wandered through the endless rows of furniture, glassware, tools, books, dolls, etc., I began dropping crumbs from a morning pastry behind me in hopes that I might be able to find my way back out again (oh why had I already eaten half of it?). The crumbs ran out in section 103, but the rooms kept coming.

I half expected to find decaying corpses of long forgotten husbands lining the walls as I searched in vain for a rest room. And then it happened, I found a wooden display case that was perfect for showing off some of my antique corkscrews. The price was marked $49.00, reasonable, but, hey this was an antique shop, so let the haggling begin. Like Diogenes looking for an honest man, I searched for an employee. When I found him, I said with conviction, "Will you take $40.00?" He looked at me as if I had just stolen his first born's future, and told me he'd have to call the dealer. You see, it seems the Emporium was one of those consignment places, where dealers display their wares, but no one in the shop can actually negotiate with you.

While the attendant disappeared into the bowels of the Emporium, Pat and I continued our expedition into the unknown. Long distance negotiating rarely works in my favor, so I began to resign myself to paying whatever the dealer offered, assuming he could be reached.

As we entered yet another musty room I began to regret not having packed a lunch, but Pat was elated to find not one but two vinegar cruets suitable for her mother's collection. But negotiating would again have to be done long distance.

Feeling much as Moses must have after several years in the desert, I saw what I thought was a mirage, but which slowly came into focus as the command center of the great Emporium. A massive desk lined with computer terminals and busy attendants wrapping fragile glassware. I approached the man who had carried the display case for me, and reminded him that I would only pay $40.00 for this treasure and not a penny more. "I spoke with the dealer," he said, "and he'll take 40 if you'll pay cash or check." Like a proud peacock spreading his wings to impress his mate, I puffed out my chest as if to say to my wife, "Look what I did. I'm THE MAN!"

Triumphantly I marched out the back door of the Emporium, head held high, feeling proud of myself, when I noticed the big sign right inside the door. It read, "20% off for cash or check." My puffed out chest suddenly found its way back down to my belt buckle. Using my high school math skills, I calculated that 20% off of $49.00 was $9.80. Everybody would have gotten that, which meant my negotiating prowess resulted in a further savings of $0.20. Part of me wanted to go back in and restart the haggling, but I knew I had lost this battle. And besides, I was out of pastry.

Antique dealers have discovered that you can avoid haggling by inserting the middle man in these consignment shops. But haggling is part of our nature. Do you ever find yourself haggling with God? Do you promise to do one thing if God will do something else for you? Do you tell God that you'll pray every day, read the Bible every night, if He will just...whatever? Have you said, "God, I'll trade you Sundays in church for a better (insert your wish here)?" Haggling with God is needless. He loves us and will do what's best for us without asking for anything in return.

And now, if you'll excuse me, there's an ice cream cake at Carvel that I think is priced too high. Let the haggling begin.

When Good Recliners Go Bad

After a generous God, a devoted wife, and loving children the most important thing in a man's life may well be his recliner. Recliners are those remarkable inventions that unlike our clothing, manage to conform to our ever changing body shape. These islands of fabric, leather and wood seem to wrap themselves around us like loving hands, cradling us in blissful comfort.

Pee Wee Herman had his "Chairy", and while I never officially named my recliner, we had a relationship forged by years of give and take. The chair would give me pleasure and comfort, while I would gratefully take every ounce of it. We did everything together: the afternoon naps; the pieces of pie, cake and ice cream enjoyed while watching hours of mind numbing television; the political conventions. When President Obama famously said "You didn't build that", I knew he couldn't mean my chair, because I had formed every wrinkle, indentation, and fold until it had become nearly an extension of my body.

My leisure life flashed before my eyes last week when the critical mechanism that formed the heart of my chair seized up like a clogged artery. It had broken a major bolt (not an easily replaced screw, but a bolt welded into place) and my beloved source of respite refused to return me to a sitting position. (Note: services will be held next week.) I needed a new chair.

Just as the search for a lost child may cause you to go to parts of town you would normally avoid, so the search for a new recliner took me to the dark underbelly of the furniture industry. A place where sales are deceptive, associates lurk in every corner armed with menacing looking clipboards, and warranties are printed in fonts so small as to render them unreadable.

First stop, a major furniture warehouse. We were lured by the massive billboard that read 50% off everything - Labor Day Weekend! Nothing held back! Who could resist? Entering the showroom we were greeted by no less than five eager sales representatives all thrusting cheaply printed business cards in our direction with the promise that they were only a cell phone call away from anywhere within the massive cavern that was the warehouse. 50% off signs were everywhere, and each piece of furniture sported two prices. The first read "Comparable Price" and the second read "Our Price." Now, I am convinced there are more people in the world who know the true location of the Holy Grail, than there are people who know someplace that actually sells stuff at the "comparable price." I want to sell my merchandise for $310.00, so I post a sign that says "Comparable Price $600.00." Who can argue?

Well, being typical consumers we assumed that "50% off" meant off of the price at which the store normally sells the item. But when I asked one of the shadows that followed us everywhere, I was informed that it meant 50% off of the "comparable price." A price that didn't exist anywhere but in the minds of the advertisers. And so the actual price was $300.00 - only $10.00 different from their normal selling price. Such a deal! As we left this den of deception, we noticed that the printed version of the billboard sign did, in fact, make that clear in type you would never be able to read at 50 miles per hour. No point in calling the lawyers.

We moved on to a second furniture den which was advertising a "Going Out of Business" sale. We actually found a chair we liked and the price seemed reasonable, but when we asked if there was a second chair (we wanted a pair) the salesman told us he thought so, but he couldn't check the inventory until we had committed to buy. This place wanted us to buy something they couldn't even say for certain they had. He did this with a straight face. Surprise - they're going out of business.

There was more, but ultimately we found ourselves at a reputable store with good prices, selling items they actually had in stock, and we weren't even given a business card by the pleasant salesperson who let us shop and test the chairs in peace.

It is in our nature as humans to be lured by the prospect of low prices, easy solutions or cheap alternatives. As we look for solutions to life's problems we may be tempted to move away from the things we know work towards empty promises and impossible dreams. But we know where the answers to our problems lie. God is the one true and dependable source for solutions and his advice is free. He doesn't tempt us with false promises or unreachable treasures. He promises simply to be with us and to guide us, and all he asks in return is our love and obedience to His word. If only God made recliners.

And now, if you'll excuse me, I've got a new recliner to break in and it's going to need a lot of loving attention.

No Appointment Necessary

Perhaps one of the biggest boons to reading ever devised is the "Doctor's Appointment." Not only does the seemingly endless time spent in the aptly named "waiting room" increase magazine subscriptions (although strangely, only for magazines with dates 12 months or older), but it encourages us all to bring books like "War and Peace" to keep us occupied during our indeterminate sentences.

The Doctor will be with you Shortly

And it seems, doesn't it, that just as we're reaching the critical juncture in our novel, or the part of the magazine article that reveals the secret to losing weight, along comes the nurse to escort you to what I fondly call the "Land that time forgot." You know, it's that little room where you're told to undress and sit on that paper covered table to wait for the Doctor who always "will be with you shortly." And invariably I'm sitting across from a full length mirror in nothing but my BVDs. A humbling experience to be sure.

I remember one time having to go to the desk to arrange for a follow up appointment. I was determined to beat the odds and get a time that would minimize my wait. I asked the receptionist, "What do I have to do to get the best possible appointment time?"

She pointed me to a clock on the wall and handed me a dart. "Take your best shot", she said. But I wasn't falling for that old trick.

"What's your first appointment of the day?" I asked. She replied, "8:30."

"Great, I'll take that," I said. But she replied, "OK, but you know the Doctor never gets in until 9."

I didn't hesitate, "Well then, give me the 9:00 appointment."

If you insist," she said, "but that will put you behind the 8:30 guy."

But there is no appointment necessary when we speak with the Holy Physician. God always makes time for us on whatever schedule we set. We can pray in the morning, afternoon, or evening. We can pray in our cars, while watching a movie, or even, dare I say it, while waiting in a doctor's office. God is on call for us 24/7. How blessed we are to know that.

And now, if you'll excuse me, I've got to locate my copy of "The Brothers Karamazov." My next appointment is coming up soon.

Creating the Perfect "Stuffy"

In the third grade I had the misfortune to have a particularly cruel art teacher. One day she looked over my shoulder at what I was drawing, and I'll never forget what she said. She said, "That doesn't look anything like a horse. Horses don't have horns, and aren't shaped like dogs." It hurt. I thought my horned horse looked pretty darned good.

Kids draw the darndest things, don't they? There's something about a child's drawing that can't be duplicated even by the most talented artist. Perhaps it's the sense of freedom that children possess that enables them to draw what they feel. Unlike we adults who have been taught better, they aren't constrained by the need for realism. If they want to draw a horse with six legs, they do. If they want to draw their little brother or sister with an eye off to one side of their head, they do it. Three fingers on a hand - no problem.

Sometimes as parents we are tempted to tell them, "But honey, birds don't have fingers. They have wings." We want to correct those little errors for fear that our kids will grow up believing that the strange creatures of their imaginations are real. I'm not so sure that would be such a bad thing, but maybe we are missing the point. Giving our children the opportunity to be creative and imaginative will pay off for them as they get older. There's plenty of time to learn proper anatomy, and the correct way to build a sky scraper.

The picture below was drawn by my daughter when she was little. It's a clown, obviously, but with a few odd refinements - note the large left leg and skinny left arm. My wife and I have an extensive collection of clowns in our "Clown Room", and this is a prized part of that display.

Recently as I was looking for a unique gift for my new granddaughter I came across the websites of some craftswomen who made stuffed creations from children's drawings. One woman called them "Stuffies". Their sites made it clear that they would not alter in any way the child's drawing. Whatever the child had drawn, that's the way the stuffy would be made.

What a wonderful idea. Rather than criticizing a child's imagination, why not celebrate it by bringing it to life.

I admit that this was a foreign concept to me. Like most parents, I wanted my child to be perfect, and my granddaughter as well. I suppose I wanted to create the perfect "stuffy." But as I looked at the photos of children who had received their stuffies, and saw the wide-eyed looks of joy at seeing their creations come to life, I realized that perfection was in the eye of the beholder.

I wanted to include a picture of the stuffy that was created from my daughter's drawing, right down to the improbable hairdo, but I couldn't pry it out of my granddaughter's hands long enough to take a shot. But it couldn't have been any more perfect.

In the hands of the great Potter we have little to fear. We know He can and will mold us to be the best. In our hands our children can also be molded, but like God, we need to be gentle as we guide them to become the best they can be. And if our child wants to put horns on a dog, well, who are we to stifle creativity? Life for our children will be full of those who will criticize and correct them. Let us celebrate their uniqueness for as long as we can.

And now, if you'll excuse me, I have to send my third grade horned horse drawing off to be made into my own stuffy.

Have You Spoken to Your Cashier Lately?

You learn a lot about people just by standing behind them in the checkout lane of a supermarket. I know, some people spend their waiting time by poking through the candy selection, or marveling at how this week's overweight TV star has managed to lose 50 pounds in just 1 week (hint: she's not poking through the candy selection at the checkout stand.) I've even found myself on occasion being drawn to plucking some gadget off the rack that boredom has convinced me I can't live without. Last week, I grabbed the last of a display of key chain lights that looked like tiny flip flops. Who could resist - their soles lit up when you pressed the little button (further convincing me flip flops are the work of the Devil.)

For the most part, though, I try to resist the myriad temptations placed at the checkout lanes. I prefer to listen to the conversations that take place at the point of sale. I sometimes think that next to a bartender, the go-to person for sharing life's problems has to be the cashier in supermarkets.

Many of us are impatient to get through the line and on to the other things we have to do, but for some, the time spent in friendly chatter with the cashier is a treasured moment. My mom was one of those older folks who just loved to talk. She lived alone for many years after my dad passed and enjoyed spending time in the local grocery store where she would share the sometimes embarrassing details of her children's lives with her favorite cashier. I knew this because on those days when I would go with her to the store, the cashier usually looked at me and said, "So, is this the son with the hemorrhoid problem you're always talking about?"

Not everyone has the family or social network that we may enjoy, and just a few moments of conversation with someone who asks about your family or your health, or what's new in your life, can turn a lonely day into one that provides a bit of comfort.

I try to be patient as I watch a lady with a walker gamely trying to fish her checkbook out of a bottomless pocketbook. Yes, some folks (like my mom did) continue to pay with checks. Kudos go to the cashiers who, I'm sure, are aware that other customers are eagerly awaiting their turn, for remaining calm and pleasant as they help less agile buyers. I try to remember that someday (all too soon) I may be the one with the walker.

But, of course, God is by far the best listener we can ever hope for. He is always interested in how we and our families are doing. His patience with our foibles is endless, and he can do so much more for us than just get our grocery bags to our cars. Say hello to Him today.

And now, if you'll excuse me, I need to thank my local cashier for her patience as I try to remove a six inch wallet jammed into a 5 inch jeans pocket.

Rolling the Pumpkins

While planning and coordinating the Great Pumpkin Festival at my church this year, I've learned more than I ever really wanted to about pumpkins. For instance, did you know that pumpkins are actually fruit? Being from the city, I'd always called them vegetables. The experts tell me that they are actually a type of berry (look it up.)

Did you know that pumpkins, despite their size and weight, are actually quite delicate? Cuts and bruises can quickly lead to decay, as can storing them in large cardboard containers (think Wal-Mart). The experts tell me that keeping pumpkins in dark places without adequate air circulation is a surefire way to promote the early demise of the fruit.

Moisture is another mortal enemy of this fall favorite. Pumpkins which are left to sit in a damp or dew laden position for too long will develop soft spots which lead to the quick deterioration of their outer skins. And so the mantra we were given when we setup our patch was, "Roll your pumpkins." Every other day, to be exact. Pumpkins on a lawn collect morning dew on the side of the pumpkins which directly contact the grass. If they are not rolled to allow the damp side to dry out, the solid looking ball of orange will eventually fall apart when picked up.

Now my wife says the same thing happens to me if I'm allowed to stay in a reclining position in front of the television for too long a period. And for that reason she often "rolls" me out of the chair to perform some home maintenance task. And I suppose there is an analogy to be made between pumpkins and humans. Both are living things which need to change position frequently to avoid becoming stale and aging before their time.

Jesus didn't insulate himself when he walked among us. He allowed himself to be enriched by seeing all sides of the human existence. He walked among the rich and poor alike, and He encouraged us to do the same. Like pumpkins, if we never turn ourselves in new directions we won't be able to remain vibrant and fresh. It's natural to find a comfortable spot and then stay there, but God wants us to grow and prosper through new experiences and by looking at the world from a different perspective.

And now, if you'll excuse me, I must respond to a 911 call from a deteriorating pumpkin in desperate need of a friendly roll.

My Binders Runneth Over

During the 2008 Presidential election, it was disclosed that while he was governor of Massachusetts Mitt Romney had put together a binder with information on women to be considered for positions in his government. Much was made in the ensuing weeks about the role of binders in American society. During the campaigning, the electorate rallied around the battle cry "A binder in every home" (conservative) or "Unbind yourselves" (liberal).

Although generally conservative by nature, I have found comfort in the thought that one day binders would no longer be needed. That we, as a people, would have moved beyond the need to categorize, to file away, to organize. That we, as the enlightened workers we are, would no longer weave a chain of vinyl covers and metal rings that, like the hapless Jacob Marley, we would be condemned to drag behind us for all eternity.

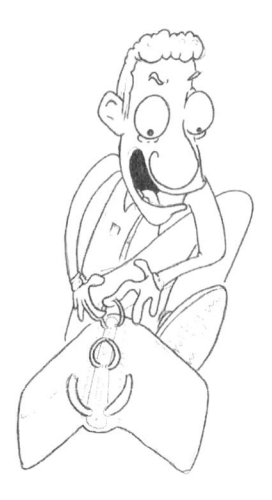

Bound to a desk for most of my professional career I was forced to endure the many indignities of cheaply made binders: vinyl that crept up from the corners of the cardboard backing; spring loaded rings that snapped ferociously at your fingers; covers that refused to stay open; pages that would never lie flat in their beds; and endless boxes of hole reinforcements licked in response to frantic office 911 calls to save paper torn asunder by cruel metal teeth.

When I retired I thought I had washed the last bit of hole reinforcement glue from my tired fingers. I vowed that being a man with years of computer experience, I would never be drawn back into the dark recesses of office closets searching for the intoxicating and addicting touch and smell of new 3 ring binders. But that was not to be. I found myself here, in the church office, home of the overstuffed binder.

On my very first day in the church office, I left a piece of myself jammed between the powerful jaws of a 6" binder as I tried to insert just one more report. I want to scan, I want to convert, I want desperately to end the tyranny of binders once and for all, but I am losing the battle. Mondays are especially good days for those who fight for binder supremacy as my desk is buried beneath piles of reports, folders of minutes, and documents without owners, each demanding a binder of its own.

Pastors, Council Officers, and members alike all want to know just one thing: where is my binder? I thought one of our AA groups might be able to help me, but their programs are all in BINDERS! And so, I ask for your prayers as I tackle the task of punching holes in 32 sets of meeting minutes from 1982 with a contraption that only handles 2 sheets at a time.

And now, if you'll excuse me, I'm expecting a large order from Staples. Let the rewards begin.

It was a dark and stormy night…

It's the classic, oft quoted, opening of many a short story and novel. And it works. Who wouldn't want to know what was going to happen next. After all, nothing good ever happens on a "dark and stormy" night, right?

This past Monday wasn't really a dark and stormy night, but it was dark and it was approaching stormy, as I sat in the church office laboring over this week's bulletin and watching the wind and rain gradually intensify.

As with all great minds, I was far too busy in recent days contemplating the many serious questions facing us (such as, why the Redskins dropped so many passes last Sunday) to think about such mundane things as sump pumps, generators, and non-perishable foods. At least that was going to be my story if disaster struck at my house.

I may be just a bit overly cynical when it comes to local television stations and their weather forecasts. There's nothing a TV station likes more than the prospect of bad weather. It guarantees them an audience and so they like to begin coverage of most storms before the storm itself even knows it's coming. And there are, of course, the ratings and advertising dollars to consider. And if it's really true people shouldn't be out and about in a storm, what are all those reporters doing standing in the middle of the road in the rain?

Once I became a believer in the power of a hurricane named Sandy, I began my search for an honest man - oops - I meant backup generator (although I would have had more success with the honest man.) Apparently, hardware stores only feel the need to stock generators during dry, sunny weather. I visited one local store and watched as a man hauled two of the rare beasts out on a cart. Finding a sales associate, I asked if there were any more. He told me they were sold out, but that he did have a carton of Charmin in aisle 13 if that would help.

At a local grocery store I found myself stocking up on SPAM. I don't even know what that stuff is, but it claims to be edible at any temperature. Milk and TP were flying off the shelves. I think I've finally made the connection. After a few days, all that milk drinking results in, well, you know, the need for all that TP. I grabbed some packs of hot dogs just in case the power went out. The plan was for my wife to grill them over her Crème Brule torch.

But our prayers were answered, and most of us in this area were spared the damage done to New York and New Jersey. God is good.

And now, if you'll excuse me, I've got to check my mailbox. I'm hoping my copy of "Making SPAM the Perfect Christmas Gift" has come in.

But honey, I'm saving money...

Normally I try to do certain things in secret, early in the morning, long before my wife has stirred from her slumber. One of those things is refilling the sugar jar. Not exactly a covert operation you might think, but, you see, it entails my hauling a 10 pound bag of granulated sugar onto the counter and removing the 2 cups or so it takes to fill the sugar jar. Then it's on to my morning breakfast of cereal which comes from an almost bottomless carton of Captain Crunch - a box so large that the cartoon character on the front is nearly life sized. Lifting it is heavy work, but the real trick is finding it behind the cases of green beans and corn which strain the shelves of our pantry.

And yes, my warehouse club card has just been renewed and my quest to save money by buying in bulk will continue throughout the holiday season.

I'm not sure what it is about buying enormous quantities of grocery and household items, but the allure of a "bonus" sized anything is difficult to resist. Why buy one light bulb when you can get a dozen for just a few dollars more? Why settle for a single box of instant potatoes when you can serve an army with the Costco special 3 pound box? And, of course, in preparation for the next Armageddon, I can stock up on 36 "Giant" rolls of my favorite toilet tissue. Who would buy just 6 rolls? Take that, Wal-Mart.

Several years ago I couldn't pass up a deal on wine gift boxes. They were incredibly cute, round containers shaped like Santa, a snowman, and a third nondescript Christmas character (perhaps an elf?) There were six in a box, and I wanted every one. I was clearing the shelves when I noticed a woman eying the final carton, but when she turned to ask her husband if she should buy it, I saw my chance, and grabbed it.

Years later, I can't hang up my winter coats because the closet is stocked with wine gift boxes. I need to find a super sale on wine and make more wine-loving friends.

Perhaps it's fear of losing out on a bargain, or our natural tendency as humans to want to be prepared for leaner times that drives us to buy more than we can use. It's good to remember that as Christians we know that God will always provide just what we need, when we need it.. And He doesn't require us to renew our membership each year.

And now, if you'll excuse me, I've got to get to Costco. I hear they're having a buy one get one free sale on jumbo croissants. There will be plenty of room in the freezer after I recycle the dozen loaves of stale french bread I bought last year.

How Do You Stuff a Tofurkey?

My children couldn't be more different. My daughter inherited a love for all forms of animal protein very early in her life, while my son apparently was abducted by a band of roaming vegetarians who indoctrinated him in the vegan way of life. Both my daughter and I have been known to salivate uncontrollably when presented with the possibility of a perfectly grilled steak, which usually causes my meat averse son to recoil in horror. And so, Thanksgiving with the kids (they're both married and in their 30's now) has become a time of blissfully stuffing ourselves while figuring out how to stuff that mass of protein known as tofurkey.

Never heard of it? Well, tofurkey (a name derived from combining tofu and turkey) is faux turkey – a loaf or casserole of vegetarian protein, usually made from tofu. Believe it or not, it is sometimes unscrupulously molded into the shape of a turkey. The terms frightening and horrifying come to mind.

Now, I can appreciate the vegan point of view even though their menu selections leave me a bit cold. But, I ask you, who are we trying to fool by forming tofu into the shapes of otherwise palatable foodstuffs? Will anyone really mistake a tofu burger for a ¼ pound of mouthwatering beef? Can a crudely shaped veggie meatball ever actually catch on with Italian food lovers? And is it even remotely possible I could ever rise in the morning with an overwhelming urge for meatless bacon?

Me, "Honey, we're out of meatless bacon! What will we do?" "

Her, "Don't worry, husband dear, we're having meatless ham tonight. ʰ, and while you're waiting, thaw out the meatless pepperoni for our ˤeless pizza. It's almost lunchtime."

ave other differences, my son and I. He's an unabashed liberal and I'm, well, I'm that party that must not be mentioned in his ˀⁱt, regardless of our differences, the Thanksgiving table at ˤge enough for everyone. We'll add an extra leaf to hold ˙ffed and ready to eat), perhaps dispense with political ˀⁿjoy watching my son-in-law devour both meat and ˀual abandon.

ally large, and he makes room for all of us. And

he does more than just tolerate our differences, He celebrates them because they come from him. It is our differences that allow us to come together as the body of Christ.

And now, if you'll excuse me, I've got to get to the store. I forgot about dessert, and I hear they are almost out of tofu ice cream cakes.

The Perils of Gift Buying

If only they loved gadgets. Women, I mean. If only they loved gadgets and toys, gift buying at Christmas time would be so much easier. Now I know there are going to be a few women out there who will protest and say, "But I love gadgets!" Wonderful, but where were you when I was in the market for a wife?

Where I am prone to want to be the first with the latest electronic doodad, my wife Pat prefers to keep things simple (the rotary dial on her cell phone still works just fine, thank you.)

Some years ago we moved from DIRECTV to FIOS. Our marriage nearly had to go to mediation when a new remote control was introduced. A year later when I ditched the FIOS contraption in favor of the latest Harmony Universal Remote, I found the Yellow Pages open to the section marked "Lawyers." A new computer? Forget about it. Moving to Windows 7 was traumatic. Windows 8 will mean a return to bachelorhood for me.

Our marriage history is rife with stories of electric can openers, trash compactors (remember those), Foodsaver vacuum sealers, cameras with more than one button and other marvels of man's ingenuity, without which my wife would have preferred to live.

Still I persist. Pat loves to read and so, in my infinite wisdom, I began a few weeks ago to gently guide her towards one of this year's must have gadgets, the Kindle Fire. It's a bit of a cross between an e-reader and a tablet. The mighty Amazon is its creator, and thanks to the Kindle app on my smartphone, I was able to give her a small demonstration of how books would work.

A little investigation showed that some of her favorite authors were available from the Kindle Store, and from their free lending library. When I threw in the prospect of checking her e-mail and (the clincher) "Angry Birds", she bowed her head in one of those feminine gestures that, I think, means "I'm not convinced, but I'm going to allow you to proceed at your own peril."

I plan to have the entire thing setup for her before she opens it. No muss, no fuss. E-mail ready to go, and the indispensable "How to Use Your Kindle Fire" downloaded and ready to read. See, honey, I'm keeping it simple for you.

God keeps it simple for us. His gift to us was straightforward. No gadgets, no setup required. We don't even have to unwrap anything. God's love and forgiveness through his Son Jesus Christ is one gift we will never need to return.

And now, if you'll excuse me, I've got to forward Pat an ad for a remote control that will allow me to control 15 devices using nothing but head movement (admittedly, fast forward is going to be a headache.)

Are we there yet?

If ever there were a phrase guaranteed to raise the hackles of adults it would have to be that ubiquitous cry of impatient children, "Are we there yet?" Next to the equally popular, "Mommy, he's touching me" refrain, it may be the best reason to forego long car trips.

But I confess to resorting to that phrase myself during this most busy time of the year. My wife and I are both involved in the Christmas production at the Port Tobacco Theater (as we were last year), and while we enjoy it immensely, the endless rehearsals, and the weekend shows that run through the middle of December, take their toll on our ability to meet other seasonal obligations. Church, pot luck dinners, pageants, family gatherings, Christmas shopping, decorating, work, sleep (I've heard about sleep), all demand a piece of the too few hours in the day.

One afternoon when I found myself without another commitment I attempted to solve the decorating dilemma by employing that age-old male practice known as simplicity. I put up the little 3 foot pre-decorated Christmas tree stored in our basement, plugged it in, and when Pat came home, proudly announced that our decorating was done. Now I know you've seen those cartoons where daggers are drawn flying from the eyes of a wife less than impressed with her husband's efforts. Well, let me tell you, they're real and they hurt. She would show me how it should be done. Fourteen boxes and 7 hours later, I was asking, "Are we there yet?"

In my younger days I used to enjoy the hustle and bustle of shopping at Christmas time, but as I've gotten older, my hustle is gone, and my bustle is considerably larger than it was. Rather than fighting the mob to get to the "deal of the day", you're more likely to find me pouring over the items hanging on the return racks. Thank heavens for the Internet. It is the great equalizer. Even the oldest and slowest of us can hold our own with the young on the World Wide Web.

Are we there yet? That is, are we at Christmas Day? Finally, we can sit back, relax, open a few presents, and admire all the work it took to get there.

It wasn't easy for those traveling to the first Christmas Day either. I wonder if Mary as she rode that donkey on the long journey to Bethlehem every said to Joseph, "Are we there yet?" But that journey was worth the effort, and as we journey towards another Christmas Day, we need to keep the final destination in mind. Our decorations, our presents, our frustrations should never cloud our remembrance of the true meaning of Christmas. God's gift to us was given freely and without condition. All we need to do is sit back, relax, and say, "Thank you, Lord."

And now, if you'll excuse me, I've got a few more boxes to bring up from the basement.

Exchanging of the Gifts - or Regifting Revisited

Have you ever regifted? Now, you can't see it in the printed bulletin, but my spell-checker is very unhappy with that word. Apparently it hasn't yet made it into the hallowed halls of Webster's Dictionary. Nevertheless, it is becoming more and more a part of the holiday gift cycle. In fact, my wife and I have been invited to an after Christmas party at a friend's house where the main event is an opportunity to unload gifts received that didn't quite fit your lifestyle or interests.

These misfit presents are tossed into a pile and during the course of the evening, following a set of rules as complex as those in the NFL, the first person (chosen by number) selects a present. The next person has the option of picking a gift from the stack, or taking the one the first person chose. If they take that person's gift, then that person gets to pick a new one from the pile. And so it goes. Bad ties are traded back and forth. Unloved cosmetics fall into the hands of those who don't need them. Tupperware lookalikes are fought over by those holding the cosmetics.

And then, by some small miracle, a gift appears that seems out of place. It's one that shouldn't be there. It's worth something, it's useful, and it shines like a beacon amidst the mountain of miscellany looking for homes. And it falls into the hands of that neighbor with the annoying dog that barks all night long. You remind yourself that you're a good Christian, think for a moment, then grab it as a small bit of revenge for those sleepless nights. But before you can savor your victory, the woman whose turn is next has snatched the object from your larcenous hands with a look that clearly says, "Remember that loud party you hosted last month?"

But perhaps the most embarrassing and best reason for avoiding these types of parties is when the item you are regifting was given to you by someone else in the crowd. Yes, I know, lime green socks are an abomination, but you should have known the preacher's wife would be at the party.

Perhaps the only saving grace to the evening is that you will leave with a treasure that can be used at next year's regifting party.

Returning gifts that simply don't fit our tastes or lifestyle seems to be an inescapable part of our Christmas experience. That's to be expected. After all, who can really know our wants, desires, and needs? Well, of course,

God can. And he answered all those criteria with the very first (and still the best) Christmas gift, his Son, Jesus Christ. A gift we will never return.

And now, if you'll excuse me, I've got a loud party to plan and I need to find a shirt to go with my lime green socks.

Defying the Laws of Aging

I know what you're thinking. That guy in the office must have been asleep by 10:00 p.m. New Year's Eve. After all, a man of his advanced seniority must require a lot of sleep just to function. And "rockin'" on New Year's Eve is just not possible.

I'll admit, my New Year's Eve experiences tend a bit more towards the Guy Lombardo end of the spectrum rather than the Pat Benatar end of Times Square. But despite an inability to understand a single word that was sung, imitate a single gyration that was performed, or even identify the name of the tune, I survived the entire Pat Benatar performance on the Fox News Channel New Year's Eve Special. Granted, I had my smartphone, my

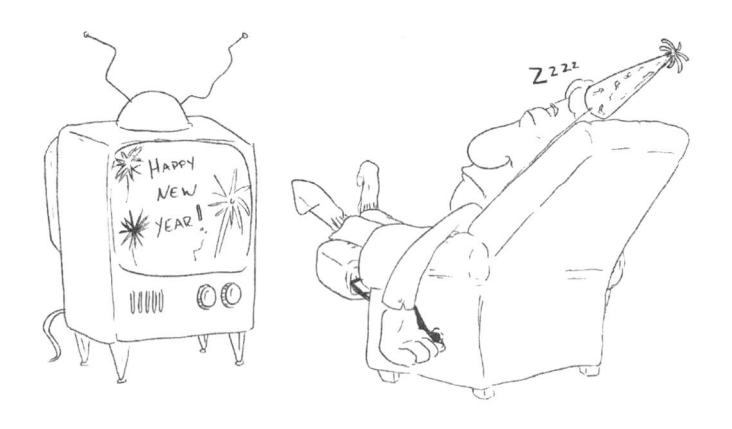

newly acquired Kindle Fire, and frequent trips to the refrigerator to assist my effort, but in the end, I beat the clock and watched the ball drop (along with my eyelids) at the stroke of midnight. When my daughter called a few minutes after midnight, I got that feeling (you know the one) that she fully expected to be leaving a message rather than speaking to dear old dad in person.

My wife Pat and I had often thought about going up to Times Square to be part of the festivities, but there is something about standing in one spot for 8 hours or more with no access to rest room facilities that just doesn't seem to be compatible with a bladder the age of mine.

Still, I don't feel old, and I don't care how many people tell me that I should. I refuse to fall behind in technology. I refuse to stop performing comedy or acting in the theater (OK, how well is subjective.) I refuse to respond to repeated requests from the Scooter Store to let them help me be mobile. I want to stay relevant in an ever changing world.

It's so easy to just sit back and exclude yourself from the world. I often find myself hitting the recliner right after lunch and not wanting to get back up again. But I do. The secret, I think, for me is being involved in as many different activities as possible (and an occasional glass of good wine - much to my mother-in-law's chagrin.)

As a new year begins, I can't say that I feel much differently than I did in the last, and that's a good thing. It means I'm still active, alive, and willing to give it another shot. I don't know if I'll be a better actor, a funnier comedian, or perhaps in need of that scooter, but it will be fun finding out.

And now, if you'll excuse me, I need to go off into a corner somewhere and sing "Auld Lang Syne", I don't think that one was in Pat Benatar's repertoire.

An aging shopper recalls the battle cry, "Remember the Cabbage Patch Kids"

I'm afraid I'm old enough to not only remember the riot inducing, pudgy-faced dolls, but to still occasionally display the remnants of a bout with CPKS (Cabbage Patch Kids Syndrome.) If you were around in 1983 and had one or more little girls, then it might well have been you I was forced to elbow aside as I fought my way towards a fresh box of the critters that had just been wheeled on to the floor of a local Sears store. I was a thinner, leaner sort back in those days, and so was no match for the crazed moms and dads who had obviously spent weeks in training for this moment. Making a rookie mistake, I tried rushing headlong into the crowd hoping to muscle my way through to the now surrounded box of dolls. They were ready for me. I felt like a mosquito buzzing around the heads of giants as arms and legs swatted and kicked me back to my starting point. It was weeks later before I stumbled upon the truck on the back lot of a shopping center. I don't know where the truck came from, and I never asked. The driver was sold out within minutes and vanished as quickly as he had come. Yes, the price was outrageous but I had scored a Cabbage

Patch Kid for my daughter.

The dolls were just the beginning. Still to come in the years ahead would be Furbys, Pound Puppies, Atari game systems, and the always annoying Strawberry Shortcake characters. My kids are grown now and so I don't follow the toy market as closely as I once did, and may not be aware of the latest craze. The toys seem to have gotten more high tech, but the procedure for getting them hasn't changed much. People will still do almost anything to get the latest and greatest. The best gifts, it seems, require us to give up our sense of decency and behave like uncivilized barbarians. Or do they?

As Christians we all know that the only true Black Friday was the day Jesus died on the cross for our sins. There were no riots that day, no major sales, no one fought to be at that scene. One man suffered on that day so that we might all gain access to the greatest gift of all. To receive this gift we have only to believe. There are no limited quantities, no rain checks to worry about, and no angry mob to face. The gift is given to us freely.

Perhaps as we go about our Christmas shopping this year, it would be wise to remember the fleeting nature of this year's toy craze. Perhaps we should share with our children the Good News of the most enduring gift ever. The gift of salvation.

And now, if you'll excuse me, there's a new American Girl doll being released at midnight, and I'm going to need a nap if I want one for my granddaughter.

The Good Old Days?

> *"Over the river and through the woods,*
> *to grandmother's house we go.*
> *The horse knows the way to carry the sleigh,*
> *through the white and drifted snow."*

What a wonderfully simple vision of Thanksgiving did Lydia Maria Child paint for us in her 1844 song. It certainly makes us long for those "good old days" when things seemed slower and easier to understand. If you tried to get to grandmother's house this past Thanksgiving using our clogged roads or our overburdened public transportation systems you might be excused if you found yourself waxing nostalgic for a sleigh and a good horse.

Whatever our age, things always seemed simpler to us when we think back to our youth. I can remember watching TV and having to wrestle with the enormous decision of which of two stations to manually tune in on our 8 inch "big" television. Of course, I had to wait until the test pattern had finished its nightly performance. We kids never fought over the remote (there wasn't one, and it was easy enough to tackle your brother if he tried to get up to change to the other channel.) I sat in my power recliner last night fiddling with my 14 device remote control, debating whether to watch one of 267 possible stations, watch a Blu-Ray movie, stream something from Amazon or Netflix, pop in a Wii game, or listen to music from any one of dozens of sources. I was exhausted and I hadn't yet pushed a button. Wrestling with all those choices can sometimes cause me to dream of those simpler times, those "good old days."

Without doubt those days gone by were simpler, but were they better? We humans have a tendency to remember things as being much better than they actually were. Did you have a favorite candy, a playground area you loved as a child, perhaps a toy that you thought was so the cat's meow (remember, we're talking nostalgia here)? I had all three, and I remember loving the multicolored candy tablets called "Smarties." I managed to find a roll of them a little while ago, and guess what? They were terrible. Too much sugar, too little flavor. Went back to that playground I loved as a child in Newark, NJ. It was still there, but was much smaller and less amazing than I had remembered it. Now, the toy, well, that one I still think was great.

In truth, I really don't want to give up the conveniences of modern life even though things would be simpler. I want my microwave, I want my smartphone, my tablet, and pop top cans. God has given us the ability to mold our futures, to make our lives better, more comfortable, and more productive. The marvels we have today could not have been imagined when I was a boy, and the marvels my granddaughter will experience will far outshine those of today.

Yesterday was simpler, but it wasn't better.

And now, if you'll excuse me, I just found a website that is selling a mint condition, barely used edition of my favorite childhood toy, Remco's "U.S.S. Hawkeye Pom Pom Gun." I still love that toy and can't wait to get it. It looks as awesome as it did when I was 6.

The Right Place at the Right Time

My mother lived in this mythical world where very young children always told the truth. When I got older, I often told her, "Mom, we lived in New Jersey not Shangri-La." But at the time, her confidence in the honesty of youth gave me an easy way to get out of trouble. My younger brother Bill helped as well, by insuring that he would always get the blame. You see, my mom had a little German blood in her, and while she was a kind and gentle person most of the time, she really didn't like it when someone argued with her. Innocent or not, Bill would consistently make the mistake of arguing his case nose to nose with her (not as hard as it sounds - mom was only 4' 9".) Me - well, saintly young thing that I was, I had learned early on that if I just kept quiet, looked sad and repentant, I'd be off the hook in no time. My excuse was generally that I was "in the wrong place at the wrong time."

My brother spent most of his childhood grounded, confined to his room, or otherwise serving one sentence or another imposed by our mom. I spent mine trying to explain to him the futility of his strategy.

As children we often do not have the luxury of picking the places we will be or the times we will be there. As we grow older we earn the freedom to make such decisions for ourselves. It's easy enough to know when we are in the wrong place at the wrong time, but how can we tell if we are in the right place at the right time? Well, for me knowing the answer to that question means being able to say "yes" to the following:

Am I happy to be there?
Do I arrive with a positive feeling?
Do I leave with a sense of accomplishment?
Did my presence make a difference to someone?
Did I laugh today?
Do I believe I am where God wants me to be?

When I think about my role here at church, I never wonder if I'm in the right place at the right time, I can truly answer "yes" to each of the questions above. It is a blessing for me to be here, and I look forward to being in the right place at the right time in the coming year.

And now, if you'll excuse me, I need to say a little thank you prayer to my brother Bill, for taking the rap for me all those years.

Resisting the Lure of Heavy Equipment

Life is constantly throwing temptations at me. It is almost impossible to escape them. I stand in line at the checkout lane in the supermarket, and find myself surrounded by candy, magazines, trinkets, and gadgets all clamoring to get into my basket. I try to direct my mind to far off places in hopes of avoiding these cleverly placed destroyers of my budget, but inevitably I awake from my daydream with a 3 Musketeers bar, or a completely unnecessary box of multicolored toothpicks in my hand.

Sometimes I'll fire up the computer and escape to an online world that I think is safer. But as I watch a viral video of Psy (Gangnam Style) performing some unrecognizable dance moves (I'm told he is "riding a horse"), my mouse seems drawn to the ever changing ads popping up next to, over and below the video. I'm told a few drops of an anti-wrinkle cream can erase years from my face (why would I want to erase all those years of hard work?) Or perhaps I'd like to buy scenic property in a valley in a state I didn't even know had valleys. I can end world hunger with a click of my mouse, or own a complete set of Chubby Checker's greatest hits (let's see, there was "The Twist", then there was...well, there was "The Twist.")

Still, I'm a big boy, and I can easily resist most of those minor temptations, but I'm losing ground to the latest attack on my self-control: Heavy Equipment. You know, Bob Cats, bulldozers, earth movers, crawler loaders, dump trucks. Now that construction has begun on our new church facility, I find myself staring into the gaping mouths of heavy equipment every morning. Their grunts and groans as they move the earth are like the call of the Sirens to me. The rumbling of their mechanized tracks cause the very earth around them to vibrate. Men are drawn to the power of these lumbering beasts, and we want to control them, bend them to our will, and, of course, crushing rocks is just a lot of fun. If the contractor ever leaves the keys in one of them.... I've had a Bob Cat on my Christmas list for the past few years, but so far, my lovely wife hasn't put it in the budget. I've often wondered why some enterprising entrepreneur hasn't opened a theme park for men featuring the opportunity to drive your own bulldozer.

I think it's about power. All of us like to think we have the power to control our lives, and those machines provide a visual representation of power. Relinquishing power doesn't come easy to many of us, yet that is what the Lord asks us to do. God wants us to put our faith in His power, not our own. Our most powerful equipment can move tons, but God can move mountains. Praying for God's direction in our lives and depending on Him is the real path to true power.

And now, if you'll excuse me, I'm renting a Bob Cat and heading for the checkout lanes at the local Safeway. I'll show those candy racks who's got willpower.

Please answer your secret security question

So there I am sitting at my computer logging into my bank account, when abruptly, without good reason, and with a menacing tone in punctuation, I was told that I must answer my secret question before I could proceed. But this isn't my first login or my first computer, I'm a veteran, and I was unafraid (after all, I only have one secret question.) I hit the enter key and up popped the question: "Last name of your first girlfriend's grandmother." What? Who? Where, when and how also raced through my mind, but didn't help. Glitch in the software, I thought to myself, then typed in the answer to what I knew was my *real* secret question. Flashing red letters alerted me to the bad news that I had answered incorrectly. It politely asked me to "try again." With absolutely no recollection of my first girlfriend (my wife Pat has always been the only girl for me), I went to the standard alternative secret question, "name of your pet." I typed it in. The letters were bigger this time, and flashing more quickly. Would Rumpelstiltskin work? Would I ever see my bank account again?

In an effort to keep us secure on the Internet, sites are asking us more and more to select and provide answers for security questions. I don't know who decides what questions you can choose from, but they must live in a different reality from mine.

One site I was trying to access wanted me to select 3 questions from a list of 5. I only knew the answers to two of the choices - I had to make something up for question 3 which was something like "Name of your pet turtle." I never had a pet turtle, but I do now. Another site wanted my mother's maiden name. Now that's not so bad but it had a limit of 8 characters. What are people with names like Chemorkovsky or those with twice hyphenated names supposed to do?

On one occasion I was happily going along with the standard mother's maiden name question, when I was told I had already used that name and could not use it again. I don't think my mother would have minded that I changed her name to "Chuckles" (the pet turtle's name - hey I've got limited memory cells to work with.)

It seems that the world is determined to protect us from accessing things improperly. Web designers and businesses want to insure that only those who are entitled to access their information can do so. The problem is that the security layers often keep those of us out who should be allowed in. But God has no such restrictions. Anyone can access Him anywhere, anytime. The only question we need to answer (and it's no secret) is do we want a relationship with Him? If only everything in life was so simple.

And now, if you'll excuse me, I'm due at the courthouse to file an official request to change my mother's maiden name to "Chuckles." It's the only way to get back into my bank account.

Did Jesus Lip-Sync the Sermon on the Mount

Not since Watergate has there been such a public outcry of indignation as that which followed Beyonce's singing of the National Anthem at the Presidential Inauguration. No, it wasn't over a wardrobe malfunction, or inappropriate gyrations. The critical issue was whether or not she had lip-synced the song as opposed to performing it live.

Ever since the early days of audio tapes, the compelling question of the day has been, "Is it live or is it Memorex?" We just had a talent show at my church. Some of the performers who sang used CD accompaniment tracks, others had a live pianist. After my performance one woman asked me if I had lip-synced the song. I told her I had not. She said, "You should have." In today's world we have a tendency to expect perfection from all those with whom we interact. We do this despite our own frequent imperfections.

And yet when someone like Beyonce gives us near perfection (her rendition of the Anthem was terrific) we focus not on the result, but only on the superficial question of whether or not she sang live in an environment that is fraught with peril for any musician. I am not among those who argue that the National Anthem is a difficult song to sing, I don't believe it is, but singing it live outdoors, in cold weather, not able to hear the music very well, and with equipment that may or may not work properly - now that's a challenge. Beyonce chose to play it safe rather than risk a poor performance at an event that was a moment of pride for the nation.

Consider Jesus delivering his Sermon on the Mount. Have you ever wondered how so many people were able to hear him? There were no microphones, no sound equipment, no recording devices, yet we are told He spoke to "multitudes".

There is a "rise" overlooking the Sea of Galilee that is often identified as the "likely" place of the Sermon on the Mount. It forms a kind of natural amphitheater where, according to those who've been there, there is a kind of natural amplification. Was this Jesus' secret, or was he just lip-syncing? Perhaps his Disciples or others were passing his words down the through the crowds. Does it really matter? After all his words were what was important.

What if God's love for us was dependent on our perfection? What if God demanded from us the same level of perfection as we demand from those who serve us? Would any of us qualify? Fortunately, God's love comes without strings attached. Perhaps we should extend the courtesy to others.

And now, if you'll excuse me, I'm prerecording my Valentine's message of unwavering love for my wife. Just can't risk a live performance.

Famous Last Words: "I think I'll just get her a card."

Men, this week's observation is primarily directed toward you (but it would be helpful if the women who happen upon it would decide to ease our burden a bit.) I'm talking about the arrival of another gift giving season - Valentine's Day, to be precise. How many of you men made the fatal mistake of believing her when she said, "Oh Honey, a card will be enough."?

I know, I know, finding the perfect gift for that perfect someone is a little bit like searching for the Holy Grail. You want to believe it's out there somewhere, but you just can't seem to put your finger on it. My gift giving efforts over the years have been woefully short of the mark. Candlelight dinners gone horribly wrong; clothing purchases that never fit; that Irish tenor who ended up sounding like Pewee Herman; the list is endless. One year I thought I had solved the problem with a unique gift of a "Rose a

Month." Wouldn't you know it, the police ran off the guy at the intersection of Route 301 & 5 where she was supposed to pick up her rose each month. I've bought all the books that purport to tell you what women really want, but apparently the authors never actually talked to any women.

One year, I thought about applying for a part time job with Hallmark. I figured if anybody would know what kind of gifts to get women, it would be those folks. I blew the job interview when I gave them the following example of my card writing skills:

Roses are red, violets are blue.
I really need this job, so hire me do.

So what's a guy to do come Valentine's Day? I have recently read several articles written by women that suggest the best thing a man can give to the woman he loves is silence. That's right guys, just shut up and listen. Resist the natural urge to solve whatever you perceive the problem to be. Just let her talk and nod your head to indicate you understand. More than anything else, this will show her you love her.

As with all things, it's probably best to look to our Lord for the right examples. When it comes to listening, God is the best. He listens and hears all that we say and feel. He doesn't interrupt, or try to shout us down. He listens intently, and in His own time guides us towards the solutions to our problems. And when it comes to showing us He loves us - well, He did, after all, give us his Son, Jesus Christ, to atone for our sins. God's gifts are always the best.

And now, if you'll excuse me, I'm going to get a box of chocolates so that we will both have something to munch on while I'm listening to my wife.

The Day the Earth Stood Still (or at least Southern Maryland)

It was an ordinary day, or so I thought. The sun was shining, there was a crispness in the air that would have sent a more sensitive person running for a winter coat, but I found it energizing. Everything seemed normal as I drove. I had the radio on and heard that Congress was still locked in battle, the President was playing golf, beer production in Milwaukee was up, and Oprah was thinking of starting yet another network. And then it happened. One of those ubiquitous "News Alerts" complete with ominous music and a trembling voice. The voice told us, with an urgency that demanded our attention that schools in Charles, St. Mary's and Calvert Counties were

closing two hours early. I found myself mentally checking my Charmin supply, as I wondered why? The voice responded to my silent question by explaining that an anonymous source driving an unidentified vehicle in an undisclosed location had reported the appearance of a snowflake, which the driver swore was unlike any other he had ever seen. Abandoning his vehicle, he risked personal safety to get this information to the authorities as quickly as possible.

Being secure in my stash of milk, bread and other essentials, my mind turned towards Davy Crockett. I wondered if he, and other pioneering Americans, would have thought twice about their exploration of the West if they had been privy to "news alerts." And, I wondered as well whether any of us could have endured the uncertainty of hitching our lives to a rickety wagon and venturing into the unknown. Would Davy and his friends view us as a bunch of "wimps" today? Would they laugh at our fear of all things natural? Would they find our expectation of being safe at all times and in all places just a bit unrealistic? It takes so little, it seems, to bring a modern society to a standstill.

In the classic Sci-Fi thriller, "The Day the Earth Stood Still", a galactic policeman tries to get the world's attention by eliminating all electrical and mechanical power. A near panic ensues. Today, all it takes is a short power outage or the threat of a snowstorm to leave us all cowering in our homes, unsure of what to do. I'm not talking about truly serious weather events like hurricanes, tsunamis and earthquakes, just the routine ones that are a part of any weather cycle. I often wonder, WWDD - what would Davy do?

It took a massive amount of faith to embark on a trip into the unknown wilderness which was the American West in the time of the pioneers. There was much to be afraid of, but our ancestors persevered through faith in their own abilities, and in the divine protection of a loving God.

Most of us will never encounter the kinds of challenges that the early pioneers had to face, but we can still look to the same loving God who has promised to care of us and see to it that we have all that we need to achieve His plan for us. We can make Davy proud by standing up to that snowflake.

And now if you'll excuse me, I need to check my collection of old Sears Catalogs.

Watching Paint Dry

Life is full of choices. From the moment we make that first painful choice to get out of that nice warm bed, we face a dizzying plethora of decisions. Granted most of our choices are relatively inconsequential - breakfast or no breakfast, bacon or sausage, matching socks or not (hey, sometimes it's hard in the dark.) But occasionally our choices can result in lost hours of productivity (or sleep).

Last Sunday night I had such a choice. I could have spent the hours from 8:30 to midnight watching paint dry, or I could watch the Oscars. I chose the Oscars, but admittedly about ten minutes into Seth McFarlane's vapid opening monologue, I found myself wandering into the den to check on the status of the paint. It was faring much better than Seth's jokes. Mercifully for Seth, the producers had Captain Kirk (William Shatner) pay a surprise visit from the future in which the Starship Captain accurately described him as "The Worst Oscar Host Ever."

In that TV world once described by Newton Minnow as a "vast wasteland", the Oscars no doubt reside in a special section reserved for shows that score lower than "My Mother the Car", and "The Jerry Springer Show" on the entertainment scale. Yes, there were beautiful dresses, and yes there were the usual mismatched tuxedo parts worn by "hip" young actors who long ago forgot how to tie a tie (much less a bow.) And yet still, millions of us watch each year as Hollywood parades its hubris across an ever more elaborate stage setting.

Life is full of choices. Each week we have to decide where we're going to grocery shop. Will it be Safeway, Giant, Food Lion, Shoppers, BJ's, Sam's Club, Costco, or the dreaded Wal-Mart? How to make the choice? Do we choose price alone? Do we look for the best selection? How about customer service? Each store has things to attract us, and things that make us want to stay away. Me? Well, I do most of the grocery shopping for our house, and I usually end up at 2 or 3 different stores each week. It seems no one outlet has everything I'm looking for.

Life is full of choices, and it can sometimes seem as if there are no easy answers. But we do have one choice in life that is a no-brainer - to follow Jesus. It's an easy choice because we know when we follow the path that Jesus has laid out for us we will receive all that we need to be happy and fulfilled. The Bible is the road map and it will take us where we need to go. And when we choose to follow Jesus, all of our other decisions will be easier to make as well.

And now, if you'll excuse me, I need to get home. I applied a second coat of paint to the den, and I know if I'm not there to watch, it will just never dry. Besides the Emmys aren't on until September.

The Real MasterCard

My wallet runneth over. Now before you jump to the conclusion that I have made a sudden leap into the ranks of the 1% targeted for additional taxes, I should clarify that the problem is not with the compartment that holds legal tender. The moths are still quite active in that section. The cause of my bulging back pocket, and tendency to lean to the left (don't worry, it's not a political thing) when walking, is the plethora of plastic "courtesy" cards that I am forced to carry. Next to the ubiquitous "Would you like fries with that?" uttered in every fast food restaurant, the most commonly heard phrase in stores these days is "Do you have your Courtesy (substitute membership, club, rewards or other) card?" Failure to present said card may result in paying full price for those bananas or that latte.

On my last trip to a local pharmacy I noticed they had my brand of soda on sale, 4 fridge packs for $10.00. Having hauled the heavy cartons to the register to check out along with my week's supply of Axe body spray, I was asked "The Question." Searching in vain, I realized I did not have the right card and was faced with paying full price (equivalent to a month's income in a small South American country) for the drinks. Not wanting to be embarrassed or thought to be cheap, I paid. I knew the savvy (and better prepared) shoppers in line behind me were shaking their heads in disbelief at the guy who paid full price for something.

Everyone from the dry cleaner to the ice cream shop wants you to carry their personal rewards cards. I now have a collection in my wallet that will someday be prized by the Smithsonian as a prime example of 21st century excess. And, it seems, I'm always just one purchase away from a free gift of some sort or another. Stores say they want to "know you", to have a personal relationship with you. Just carry our card and we'll give you reasonable prices on our products. Here's a quick suggestion, instead of dozens of separate cards, why not have some kind of Unicard. When you wanted to join a store's rewards or member program, the store could simply add its unique identifier to the data on the card. Safeway, Giant, CVS, Food Lion, Walgreens - all on one plastic card. The card readers at each store could easily handle this kind of integration.

Stores spend millions of dollars collecting information on us, they say to better serve our needs. But do they ever really get to know us? The real MasterCard, and the only rewards card we ever need is the one Jesus gave us with his death on the cross. Our father in heaven knows every hair on our head, his rewards are everlasting and it doesn't even take up a slot in our wallets.

And now, if you'll excuse me, I have an appointment with my chiropractor. He has suggested moving my wallet to the right pocket to restore some balance in my posture. And, as a bonus, he invited me to join his "Preferred Patient Program" complete with plastic membership card.

The Undiscovered Easter Egg

Things get misplaced in our house all the time. Between my wife Pat and me, we could keep a dedicated team of Lost and Found professionals busy full time. I'm a creature of habit (which explains why I continually make the same mistakes - just check with the bulletin editors that help me each week.) If it's not a lost pair of glasses, it may be a misplaced cell phone. Unsolicited and unnecessary digression: Did you know that most of the newer smart phones have a "scream" feature that can allow you to remotely cause your phone to emit a high pitched noise that would rouse the dead or help you find your lost phone?

I lose track of my car keys all the time. I have a small flash drive attached to the key chain, and I often plug the drive into my computer at home to transfer a file but fail to remove it, and therefore when I next go to start my car, the keys have vanished. I always find them again, but not until many minutes have passed and some head banging has taken place.

Has this ever happened to you? You dutifully hide colorful eggs on Easter morning for the kids to find. A good time is had by all. But you feel something is missing. Then, some months (or in my case years) later, in a long forgotten desolate corner of the house, you discover the one egg you failed to locate that Easter of 1985. The amazing thing is that it looks almost as good as the day you hid it.

Now you have no intention of eating it or giving it a place of honor on the fireplace mantle, but none the less there is that momentary feeling that mimics the joy of the Prodigal Son's coming home. You are filled with the reminders of a wonderful time when the children were young, life seemed simpler, and it was all about finding those eggs.

Computer games and software often contain secret "goodies" called Easter eggs. These are fun little additions, added by programmers, which can be found "accidentally", by completing some tasks, or by hearing about them from other people. They are unexpected, fun and elicit reactions similar to the one my wife has when she comes home to find I've done the laundry.

We are never too old to experience the joy of Easter eggs. I wonder if we can imagine the immense wonder and excitement that came with the very first Easter surprise. When the women went to the tomb to find it empty, and then learned that Jesus had risen from the dead. And as the word spread of the risen Lord, so did the excitement and joy. And it continues today on this Easter Sunday as we once again are reminded of the gift of salvation provided by Jesus to all who accept his grace. Alleluia! He is Risen!

And now, if you'll excuse me, I've got some salad to make with a couple of lost eggs that have been found. Pray for me.

Dan wants to kill Jiminy Cricket

Well, maybe "kill" is a bit strong, but occasionally I do get the urge to silence the little critter - don't you? We each have our own Jiminy Cricket, that little voice inside our head that reminds us when we are thinking of straying from the path that's been set for us. It's that voice that chides us when we are about to ignore a resolution we've set for ourselves. And when it happens on April 1, it just seems that much more like a bad joke.

God is good. You'll get no argument from me on that count. But life can be cruel. This is especially true when two very worthy goals are suddenly in conflict. It was Easter morning, and as I grunted and groaned trying mightily to squeeze my misshapen body into a handsome suit of clothes from an earlier era in my life I gave up in frustration and instead slipped into what can only be described as the male version of a mumu.

As I stood with the choir that morning singing our Easter Cantata, my constricted waist cried "Enough!" I vowed to start the dreaded *diet* Monday morning. And now the cruel part. After weeks of praying, begging and otherwise trying to mooch, borrow, or obtain through less than idyllic means my two favorite Easter treats, (the always necessary vanilla butter cream egg, and Russell Stover's Marshmallow eggs) both showed up in my Easter Basket (yes, I have an Easter Basket - wanta make something of it?) And that's when Jiminy made his appearance.

Monday came, and staring into the basket of longed-for goodies my hand slowly inched towards the Vanilla Butter Cream Egg (on its way it hovered, trembling, for a moment, over the marshmallow eggs), and then that annoying little bug began his finger pointing and lecturing about the promise I had made only hours earlier. "Remember the suit," he chided. "Picture that mumu on Facebook", he threatened. I wondered, for just a brief moment, if you could kill a cricket by dropping a vanilla butter cream egg on him.

"But," I protested, "My daughter just brought me 4 bags of my favorite potato chips. Think of the waste!" But Jiminy was unmoved. "Exactly," he replied, "think of the "waist." He was right. God is forgiving and kind - crickets, not so much.

"Well," I countered, "I suppose if I eat one of those eggs you'll make my nose grow another inch." I said derisively. "No," the little wise guy cracked, "but I will add an inch to your already bulging belly." That did it. The thought of having to up-size my mumu was too much. The cricket had won. The diet would begin on schedule.

Our struggles with the challenges of this life can seem enormous to us. But as we remember the life and death of Jesus, the temptations He faced, the painful and difficult choices He made - all for our salvation - we can gain the courage to face our own demons. Jesus had the voice of God to bring him comfort and guidance. We too, can have that same voice and it will give us the strength to achieve those things that are best for us.

And now, if you'll excuse me, I promised a certain cricket I would get him a new hat and umbrella.

Dan Goes to the Circus

The Piccadilly Circus was in town this past weekend. They had set up their tent in an area adjacent to National Harbor and Pat and I had tickets for the front row. With just one ring and a single elephant (not me, I am dieting, you know), this show posed no threat to Ringling Brothers, but just the same, they put on a pretty decent show.

The Midway left a bit to be desired, as it consisted only of rides on your choice of a camel, pony, or elephant. No sword swallowers, or fire eaters; not even a bearded lady (although I did see one gal with a bit of a mustache.) Even the concessions were minimal, sporting only funnel cakes (curse that diet), snow cones and popcorn. Important financial note: you needed your checkbook, credit card, proof of home ownership, as well as a co-signer to be able to afford the concessions. In fact, the prices were so high I considered slipping out to a movie theater to get a better price on soda and popcorn.

Once the show started, the performers were really quite good. The opening act was a man who walked on the inside and outside of a giant steel wheel. There were jugglers (actually quite amazing jugglers), tumblers, clowns, aerial acrobats, and a very talented elephant with a personality.

Now here's the really interesting part: It became obvious after a couple of acts that the members of this circus troupe played multiple roles. Virtually all of the performers reappeared at least once with a second completely different act. And sometimes they would show up yet again to assist other acts or perhaps just to move equipment. Imagine our surprise when one of the aerial acrobats showed up during intermission to set up an instant face painting station. And while I can't prove it, I could swear that funnel cake guy was one of the tumblers. When a very attractive young lady in a gorgeous sequined outfit strolled into the ring to take a bow, Pat turned to me and said, "Hey, isn't that the girl who showed us to our seats?" It was. As it turned out the whole circus troupe couldn't have been more than 20 or 25 people, each serving multiple roles and demonstrating multiple skills.

God gives us all the ability to do many different things. We may feel that one skill is dominant and make that our focus, but we should never forget that He has given us a variety of talents. Our job should be to identify those talents, and seek to use them as often as we can. Life may be a circus sometimes, but we can make it a successful show.

And now, if you'll excuse me there are 8 bowling pins waiting to be juggled. Take cover.

Dan longs to look like his caricature

My wife Pat is afraid that people will think she doesn't have a husband. I'm not talking about just when it's time to do the dishes, or wash the clothes, or vacuum the floors (we have floors?). She's upset that I am always the one taking the pictures on our trips, but never appear in any of them. Note to those wishing to avoid being in pictures: I wisely insisted on buying complicated camera equipment with long boring user manuals to insure that only I would know how to properly operate the devices. It's not that I have this desire to remain forever anonymous, it's just that I've never liked the way I look in photographs. When I was a child I was skinny as a rail (oh, to revisit childhood) and embarrassed by that. Today I look more like a locomotive, and I don't mean sleek, fast and proud (think steam locomotive).

We had a church directory picture done recently, and I made the huge mistake of buying the picture without the expensive "touch-up" work offered by the photographer. Pat looks great, but I appear to be someone who was on his way to audition for the role of extra in the popular AMC series "The Walking Dead." I recently changed my primary physician because I finally found one who didn't badger me about my weight every time I see him (although I'm not sure what he meant by the phrase "Easy, big fellow" when I jumped onto the scale).

When I was younger I admit to being a bit more obsessed with my appearance, but as I got older I realized that my body and my wallet were not going to be able to keep up with the latest trends in fashion. I think back fondly to the days when Pat and I got married and were slim and trim. On our honeymoon, she looked great in her bathing suit, and I wore something that today I couldn't even get over my ankles. When I first began exploring stand-up comedy, I had a caricature done that I thought would be useful for advertising purposes. Now, when anyone asks for a picture of me, I send them that drawing. It looks much better than the real thing. I'm practical though, I never buy products that guarantee to make me look years younger. What I need is something to make me look decades younger.

At a dog show recently I observed the proud owner of a Mexican Hairless. To most, this less than photogenic species would probably be considered ugly, but to the man who called him his companion and friend, the dog was a thing of beauty. Beauty is indeed in the eye of the beholder, and to our Father in Heaven, each of us is a beautiful example of His divine vision. God looks to influence our minds and our hearts, and when we follow His plan for our lives, we take on a beauty that far surpasses our physical limitations.

And now, if you'll excuse me, QVC has an anti-wrinkle cream available by the pound. I'll be ordering a case and looking up the phone number of a good caricature artist.

The Uncomfortable Intrusions of Social Media

I consider myself computer and tech savvy, and perhaps even a little "hip" for my age (did I just blow that assessment by using terminology from the 60's?) I don't tweet (at least not in polite company), but I do use Facebook, occasionally instant messaging, and I've even been known to SKYPE once in a while. My understanding of Internet shorthand is pretty much limited to ROFL (rolling on the floor laughing), but I do have access to an under 20 type who will translate for me when necessary. Facebook started out as a great way to stay in touch with the lives of people you might not see in person very often, but I think it's beginning to lose its way.

My Facebook feed is overloaded on a daily basis with pictures of what people had for breakfast, what they're thinking about having for lunch, and the potluck wonders created for church suppers. A lot of bad meals are showing up regularly. One friend, who is on some sort of extraterrestrial health diet, publishes color photos of meals that look like a cross between road kill and six month old humus. I suppose he's hoping people will tell him how yummy it looks so he'll feel better about eating it.

And Facebook is constantly prodding me to "share" information that I might consider private with the rest of the Facebook community. I'm often reminded that friend "A" is sharing that he walked his dog in a particular park, or friend "B" is checking in from the railroad station (maybe he thinks I know where his ticket is). Then there's friend "C" who thinks I need to know that she vacuumed her living room carpet while practicing the violin. And if Facebook doesn't think you're sharing enough, it will prompt you to expand your postings. This morning I logged on and got this popup message: "Would you like to share your colonoscopy results with your Facebook Friends?" No, I would not, thank you. But not wanting to seem completely antisocial, I did post that my schizophrenia medication seemed to be working.

It's important to keep in touch with our friends, and it is fun to know what's going on in their lives, but there are limits to what we are willing to share with the world. That's where prayer comes in. When we pray we are speaking to a friend with whom we can share our most intimate thoughts, our heaviest burdens. God wants to hear about our successes and our failures, and when God "comments" on something we've shared with Him, we can be confident that it will be advice we can trust. Our Father is on a 24/7 chat line. He's always available, always has time for us, and will always listen without interrupting. And He will never "unfriend" us.

And now, if you'll excuse me, I have it on good authority that friend "D" will be posting his cholesterol levels in a few moments, and I've got some dietary tips for him.

An Indispensable Tool for Dieting

She, who must be obeyed (for those of you not up on the 1965 Ursula Andress movie of the same name that would be a powerful woman - my wife) has decreed that we must lose weight.

Now in the movie, Ursula Andress plays Ayesha, the beautiful Queen of a lost civilization, whose love holds the promise of immortality. My wife has not promised me immortality, but she did say I'd live to see another day if I joined her quest for a healthier life style. Somehow my encounters with chocolate cream pies, pizza, cheesecake and other late night snacks were making it harder for her to concentrate on her rice cakes. And so, I have given up many a glorious pastry to support our now common goal.

And it's working. Just today, for example, I went from wearing a size 42 jeans to a size 40. Surprisingly, scratching out that 42 with a magic marker wasn't as hard as I thought it would be. Serious progress will be noted when the bathroom scale no longer displays "continued on next scale" when I step on.

In an age where technological marvels are available to assist us with almost any effort, it's sometimes comforting to know that simple devices still have a place in our tool kits. Of course, we all know that a magic marker is not the real secret to losing weight. It really doesn't matter if you are going low fat, low carb, low calorie or some other approach; at the end of the day it always seems to come down to willpower. 9:00 pm is my weak moment of the day. By that time I am generally done for the day and relaxing in that recliner that does everything but massage my overstuffed body. And boy, do I want something to snack on.

Temptation is everywhere. The TV is spitting out commercials for cheese laden pizzas, followed by the latest episode of "Cupcake Wars". I go to the fridge - just to browse mind you - only to be faced with shelves full of uneaten treats. And then the unkindest cut of all: news that Twinkies will be resuming production at the end of July. I scream, "Get thee behind me Hostess!"

And I return to the recliner with a piece of string cheese or a can of lite fruit. Another small victory in the ongoing war against weight. But willpower alone may not be enough. I am weak and ready to accept almost any excuse to stray from my dietary goals. But fortunately I do not have to go it alone. I have my wife to support me, as I try to support her. And we both have faith that the Lord will give us both strength to face this challenge, just as He has in facing so many other challenges over the years. Thank you Lord, for always guiding us to do what is best.

And now, if you'll excuse me, I have to write a letter to Hostess apologizing for the negative effect my diet is going to have on their bottom line.

Warning! Warning! Geek Alert!
Content May Not Be of Interest to Normal People

I have been involved with computers for as long as I can remember. My very first (do you ever forget your first?) was an Atari XE model - a pretty slick 8bit machine for its day. I nixed the Commodore line which was popular, just because it was popular. Atari later came out with a 64bit model and I thought I had reached the ultimate in home computing power. Even today I am amazed at what I was able to do with so little memory (the computer, not my brain) and absolutely no external storage. But computers continued to evolve, and I soon had a brand spanking new Kaypro II which came with its own monitor and, "drum role", a 5 ¼" floppy disk drive (yes, children, they did make disks that large back in the day.) Internal hard drives would follow, smaller solid disks (we still called them "floppy" for some reason), ZIP drives (still have some of those), and the list goes on.

Today we have massive hard drives, gigabytes of computer memory, flash/thumb drives, HD monitors. The operating systems have moved from the black or green days of MSDOS and cryptic commands, to sleek, colorful interfaces culminating in the latest Microsoft version, Windows 8, with its tiles and touch screen capabilities. Breaking news: Windows 10 has arrived and I'm converting as I type this.

And yet, with all this power, there are still people typing with one finger. This past weekend I set up a new computer for my mother-in-law. I had to do it. Got tired of every time I visited, having to field calls from the Smithsonian asking if she was ready to donate her Paleolithic model. Computers are wonderful and our world would not be as interesting without them, but they are only as useful as the people who use them. She is still typing with one finger, but the results look so much better on her new HD monitor.

With all the power of modern computers, we humans still are bound by our own limitations. Despite gigabytes of memory, I still can't remember where I put my car keys. But God knows, just as He knows the number of hairs on our heads (or follicles in some cases.)

Unlike computers, God has created us to be infinite in our capabilities and our ability to absorb knowledge and learn. God is the ultimate help desk, the master tech support resource. Got a problem? Can't make an important decision? God is available to CHAT 24/7. Just mentally click on that little button in your brain marked "Prayer", and take your problems to Him.

And now, if you'll excuse me, I have to call my mother-in-law. She says she misplaced the "Windows Key" on her keyboard, and can't put her one finger on it.

Remembering Mom in the Checkout Lane

Are you thinking of your mom today? Me too. My mom's been gone a few years now, but I can't walk into a grocery store without thinking about her. If that sounds strange to you, it's only because you never went grocery shopping with Johanna Brennan. I don't know if they put pictures of notorious customers on the walls of the offices in the secret upper levels of grocery stores, but if they do, then my mom's would have been a huge 11x14 glossy print in full color. My mom loved grocery stores. When she was physically able she would walk down to the local Safeway, but as she grew older her lack of mobility required that someone take her. That job often fell to me.

My mom needed help in the grocery stores - no, not because her eyesight was poor, and not because she had to rely on the shopping cart to help her stay upright. Mom just liked the attention she got when she would waylay some unsuspecting clerk to help her find the most difficult to locate item in the store. It wasn't unusual to find two or more clerks madly scrambling to meet her demands. And she didn't always wait for someone to wander by. Despite her slight frame at 4" 9", she had the voice of a ring announcer at a heavyweight boxing match. "Can someone help me!" she would boom from the middle of an aisle. "I can't find my TAB." Yes, my friends, she was the last person still drinking that failed version of diet cola.

I always offered to help, but she wouldn't hear of it. She would tell me to go away, that she could handle things herself. As soon as I turned the corner, I'd hear, "Can somebody help me?" Believe it or not, the folks who worked at Safeway and Giant loved her.

When it came time to check out, I desperately tried to find a lane as far away from hers as possible. You see, my mother thought of the checkout clerk as the next best thing to a priest in a confessional. She'd tell them anything. "Oh, that anti-itch ointment is for my son, he's always scratching." "No, I don't need Pepto Bismol. My son has a stomach problem." Once when I was in lane 10 and she was in lane 1, she spotted me. I tried to duck down behind the magazines, but she saw me and yelled for all the world to hear, "Danny! Danny! I found that Preparation H you were looking for. Got you the large tube."

She didn't really do it to embarrass me. She really didn't see anything to be embarrassed about. Now when I check out, the clerk always asks me, "Did you forget the Preparation H?"

But this Mother's Day, do you know what I wish more than anything? I wish I could hear her voice once again in the grocery store calling out my name. God gives us our moms on this earth for a period of time, but the memories are forever. What are you thinking about your mom today?

And now, if you'll excuse me, I've got some shopping to do, and some memories to enjoy.

Dan Discovers The Root of All Evil

And so it was bound to happen. The signs were all there. I had received my Scooter Store certificate, a complimentary membership in Seniors United (a group dedicated to the preservation of mahjong), a free six-month supply of glucosamine chondroitin, and a Barry Manilow album. Alright already, I'm getting old. I get it. Stop reminding me with free Reader's Digest subscriptions.

But somehow I could always take comfort in knowing that I still had my hair. Yes, it's white as snow, but otherwise it's healthy as a horse. Well apparently not. The latest advertising now informs me that I may be suffering from something called "aging follicles." This results in follicular depletion - and you know where that ends up, right? But fortunately, modern science (or quackery) is alive and well. There is no shortage of products to help battle the miscreant follicles that are committing Hara-Kari under my scalp. I can rub stuff onto my scalp; I can massage the little demons with pulsating electric fingers, I can play soothing music to calm them; and I can even try to replace them with cousins from other parts of my body (will I need to use deodorant?)

None of that stuff for me. Not when I found the little device pictured at the right on E-Bay. It's called the "Thermocap", and was developed in 1925 by The Allied Merke Institute in New York City. This little beauty claims to stimulate circulation, cleanse clogged-up pores, and nourish dormant hair bulbs. It seemed the least I could do for my aging follicles. And all I have to do is sit there and let it do its work.

We humans obsess over the most unimportant things. We worry about our height, our weight, whether or not we are handsome enough or beautiful. We worry about our status, our wealth, and our possessions. We worry if we are as important or as good as the next person.

Luke 12, verse 7 reminds us: *And the very hairs on your head are all numbered. So don't be afraid; you are more valuable to God than a whole flock of sparrows.* As we go about God's work in our lives, we need not worry about anyone or anything else. God has our back. He knows our needs and will provide for them.

And now, if you'll excuse me, I need to get to the barbershop. It seems the Thermocap has done its work and my follicles are alive and better than ever.

Remember the Date?

I enjoy irony, which is why I found the headline of a column in a recent edition of "The Maryland Independent" and its accompanying first sentence so amusing. The headline read "**Remember the Date**". The first sentence was, "National Memory Screening Day will be ...." Let's see, I'm thinking of having my memory screened because I might have problems remembering, so all they want me to do is *remember* the date of the screening.

Now, what was I saying, oh yes, forgetfulness, that's right. It's no secret that as we get older our memory capacity seems to shrink just a bit. A good friend of mine, a retired pastor, was always known for his ability to

remember names. He could recall the names of anyone he had ever met, and was often fond of pointing people out to me as they came into church on Sundays. Sadly, in recent years he's lost a bit of that edge. Now my wife, ah...let's see, her name is...don't tell me, it starts with a "P", yes Pat, will tell you that my memory can be a bit faulty at times. Birthdays, anniversaries, names, places, I treat them all equally. That is to say, I tend to forget them all.

141

My memory limits are most apparent when I'm behind the wheel and trying to navigate to somewhere I have not been to at least 100 times. Do I turn right, left, go straight ahead? Am I even in the right state? One of the greatest gifts I have ever been given is a Garmin GPS. Without it I'm not sure I would make it home some days. There's something comforting about that firm, assertive voice announcing "RECALCULATING" when I've made a wrong turn. I think my GPS has the ability to learn as it seems to have added "AGAIN" to its "RECALCULATING" warning. Can a GPS get angry?

To overcome my ability to forget where things are, I have developed a strict regimen of putting my keys, glasses, wallet, etc., in the same place every day. On those rare occasions when I am distracted and don't follow the protocol, I generally just take the day off.

These are, of course, trivial matters, but how we live our daily lives is much more important. Remembering who we are, what we believe, and how we should be navigating the pathway of life, these are vital to our well-being.

Sometimes we Christians get so caught up in the many things that demand our time and attention, that we forget what it really means to be a follower of Christ. But God gave us the very first GPS (God Provided Script) to show us the way. It's called the *Bible*. When we get a little lost in this complex world, the answers are always there for us. We just need to open the book.

And now, if you'll excuse me, I need to get my GPS a cup of coffee. It seems a bit frustrated.

Heckling as an Art Form

As a part-time, aspiring stand-up comedian, I learned very early on that you have to be able to handle hecklers. Sooner or later you'll run into one. But there are proven methods for surviving the amateurish efforts of hecklers to embarrass you. Or so the professionals would have you believe. Of course, the professionals had never met my mother.

My mom was the source of much of my humor, and, to be honest, I don't think she liked the competition. Invariably, she would seat herself in the front row of a show I was doing, and would waste no time warming up the audience for me. As I would step out onto the stage, I could hear her mutter loudly enough for the first several rows to hear, "I hope he's not going to tell those same old jokes again." Apparently my mom assumed I would always have fresh material, and would never use the same jokes twice. Most hecklers are frowned upon by audiences, but my mother elevated heckling to the status of an art form. Often she got more laughs than did I. To be fair, I didn't hesitate to use my mom as the inspiration for many of my routines, and I know that both of us enjoyed the "sparring" from time to time.

My comedy often has me as the target (it's called self-deprecating humor). Once while addressing a group of Verizon employees before a team building exercise, I was using that technique. Afterwards my co-instructor seemed visibly upset that I would make fun of myself. I just told her it was better to beat the hecklers to the punch. Let's face it, if you can't laugh at yourself, who can you laugh at?

Each of us faces our own hecklers in life. Perhaps it's someone at a meeting you are running who continually interrupts or challenges your every thought. Perhaps you've been out to dinner with your family, paused to say grace and noticed that others in the restaurant were looking at you strangely or muttering comments about your behavior. Hecklers are all around us.

Jesus encountered more than His share of hecklers. Wherever He went there were always those who wanted to challenge Him. He was frequently heckled by the priests and Pharisees in an effort to get Him to say something that could be used against Him. We know the Devil and other demons taunted, tempted and heckled Him. Jesus knew how to deal with hecklers. He didn't ignore them, but often turned the encounter into a teachable moment. That's just another wise lesson Jesus wants us all to learn.

And now, if you'll excuse me, I need to prepare. I have this fear that one day I'll be standing at the pearly gates pleading my case to St. Peter, and my mom will be there heckling from behind the gates.

A Square Peg, a Round Hole and Me

Remember that old test where you had to fit different shaped pegs into the proper openings in a board? You know, the old, trying to fit a square peg into a round hole routine. I have often been seen desperately pounding a peg into a hole it was never intended to fit into. Fortunately, I have an understanding wife who doesn't have a problem walking up to me and saying, "You know, if you just turned it around the other way, it would fit fine."

To me the most brilliant people in the universe are not rocket scientists, genetic engineers, thoracic surgeons, or philosophers. After all, they are only dealing with simple things like nuclear fission, ion propulsion, the meaning of life, or the functioning of our hearts. No, the most brilliant people in the universe are Packaging Designers. Those are the people who figure out how to get products into packages that were intentionally made to be too small.

If you've ever had to return a product, then you've experienced the struggle to get the item back into its original packaging. I am convinced these packages are engineered to shrink at the molecular sub particle level so that they are only 1/3 their original size. This happens automatically when a product is removed from its packaging. I recently had to return a tower computer to the manufacturer for repairs. The company provided the box for me. It looked deceptively simple. Just insert the precut foam pieces into the box, set the tower into them and seal the box. Do you have any idea how many ways a piece of precut foam can be inserted into a box? I do. I turned and twisted, and bent and shaped that piece of foam, but there was no way the tower was going to fit in the space provided. Normally I'm not allowed to use sharp implements, but I grabbed a knife and began hacking away (I say "hacking", because any other word would imply that I knew what I was doing). The final score was: foam 1, me 0. Still, I wedged it in there somehow.

Just last week we were evaluating new telephone instruments for the church offices. I had very carefully unpacked one telephone creating a mental picture of where each part had come from as I pulled it out of the very tight box. We decided against that particular model, and I tried to repack it. If only my brain were a DVR. I could have rewound the extraction process. As it was, I believe I created a new life form while jamming the pieces back in the box (I knew it was alive because the pieces kept jumping back out at me.)

As amazing as the complexity of our human products may be, they pale in comparison to the complexity of God's universe. Just look at the brilliant packages He calls His children. I think sometimes that's what God is trying to do with us - get us back into our original packaging.

And now, if you'll excuse me, I've got a home gym I need to repack.

Dressing for Success

It's all about the candy. Every kid knows (or should) that the better the costume, the greater the haul. When I was little, I knew what I wanted to be for Halloween. A soldier, a policeman, a fireman, Charles Atlas (I was so skinny, I dreamed of putting on enough weight to become a 97-pound weakling). Those were the heroes back in the day. Oh sure, there was Superman, and I would have been all right with that costume as well, but you see, my mother, talented though she was, had no facility for designing Halloween costumes. Her repertoire of ideas consisted of Little Bo Peep and a Hobo. The problem was that my brother and I both needed costumes, and so...wait for it...every year one of us was Little Bo Peep and one of us was the Hobo. We alternated. I hated being the Hobo, but comforted myself in knowing that it was a step up from the shepherdess.

These days I don't have that problem. My wife Pat is an extremely creative costumer. Having a 1776 party, we're there. Invitation to a 1920's speakeasy jam, no problem, just give us a minute. Need a headless horseman in a hurry, don't fret, we're ready to go. The irony is, now that I have the costumes that would guarantee me a great candy haul, I'm on a

147

diet! Life can be so unfair.

In her last years with us, my mom loved to dress up and sit outside of our garage on Halloween night. She enjoyed the little children and their imaginative costumes, and was a bit less pleasant with those older kids who didn't bother to dress at all. And I had a bit of sweet revenge. You see, the costume that Pat had for my mom looked (at least to me) an awfully lot like a certain Little Bo Peep (although in her waning years.)

Dressing up and pretending to be someone else in some other time or place, is something that we never outgrow. It gives us the freedom, for a short time, to escape our problems and frustrations. That's a good thing, but we also know that reality is still out there waiting for us. And that's when our relationship with Christ really pays us dividends. Our Lord knows just who we are and He never asks us to be anything other than ourselves. When we pray (think talk with Him), we have no need to disguise our wants and needs. There is a true sense of freedom in the honesty of prayer to the Lord.

And now, if you'll excuse me, I'm off to dust of my old costume. I understand the Hobo look is coming back into style.

Multitasking - Not Always a Good Thing

When I began my career with the telephone company in the early 70's (no, not the 1870's), my first assignment might well have been my last. In those days anyone working in the residential end of the company was required to spend three months as a Service Representative in the Business Office to learn the fundamentals.

There were no computers or other devices as this was the era of paper records. Customer records were filed throughout the office in file drawers (remember those?). To be a Service Rep at the phone company meant you had to be able to multitask. You had to be able to talk to the customer, pull and file paper records, and write service orders all at the same time. Now talking with the customer came easily for me, but filing or writing at the same time - that didn't happen. In fact, if it hadn't been for the women around me (at that time I was the only male in the office), I would have had a very short career. They were multitaskers of the first degree and put their filing skills to work helping me.

Webster's Dictionary defines multitasking as "the ability to do several things at the same time." That can be a valuable skill in certain professions, but it's not always a good thing. Sometimes we need to focus on a specific task in order to avoid those 'unintended consequences" that pastors often warn us about.

My wife and I have been attending the Maryland Renaissance Festival for more than 24 years. My collection of souvenir mugs includes one for each of those years. We always attend in period costume, and I take one of the mugs from a prior year to use for whatever I may be drinking that day.

This year I had a mug from 2004, and I had purchased the 2013 mug. On the trip home, both were in my trunk safely underneath pieces of our costumes. Once home, always anxious to show off my multitasking skill set (and not wanting to make two trips), I grabbed a stack of our clothes, and as I yanked them out of the trunk, I watched helplessly, in what seemed like slow motion, as the new mug was pulled out of the trunk and hit the garage floor with a heart stopping crash.

Never one to learn from a mistake, I returned to the trunk grabbed more bags and my old mug. With both hands I foolishly tried to close the trunk. As if I were watching a DVR replay, my prized 2004 mug was knocked from my hand and hit virtually the same spot as its newer brother. I should have focused.

When you pray, do you multitask? Are you thinking about your plans for the rest of the day, or the work week coming up? Are you thinking about how hot or cold it is, how much you've still got to do? Or, do you give your full attention to God and your conversation with Him? There are times when we need to focus, prayer is one of those times.

And now, if you'll excuse me, I'm desperate to find a replacement 2004 Renaissance mug.

Memory - all alone in the moonlight...

The Pastor at my church recently gave a sermon titled "I'm Singing in the Pain." I'm not sure if the pastor realized it or not, but most of the congregation spent the duration of his sermon silently humming the tune from "I'm Singing in the Rain". You're probably already humming the melody yourself right now. No need to thank me, as it will probably be in your head for most of the day. It's one of those tunes that embeds itself in a portion of the brain over which we seem to have no control.

Now, it's not particularly embarrassing for people to find you humming a great song like that, but if you're me, the songs my aging brain chooses to remember are less lofty. My problem is advertising jingles. As inane as they are, the unscrupulous creators of these little ditties know just how to trick your mind into recalling them at the oddest times. Listening to the radio in the morning I often hear a jingle from a charitable organization wanting you to donate your car. It's "1 877 KARS for KIDS". Sing it with me now:

"One eight seven seven KARS for KIDS,
K A R S , KARS for KIDS.
One eight seven seven KARS for KIDS,
donate your car today."

Not sure how the tune goes? Well, stop by the office and I'll gladly infect you with it.

Of course, I'm showing my age (you wouldn't have noticed otherwise, right?) So many of today's commercials rely on more modern musical themes which may or may not have a melody you can actually remember. That's unlike classics like this one which begins, "My Bologna Has a First Name it's _ _ _ _ _..." Bet you can guess what that name is, and bet you are stuck with the jingle for the rest of the day. Oh, if you're having trouble, try that company's other famous jingle "Oh, I wish I were an ____ ____ wiener..." (fill in the blanks.) Uh, oh, there goes my afternoon.

Jingles serve a very important purpose in the advertising world. They compel us to remember products in which we might otherwise have no interest. And when we hum or sing them, we are providing free product marketing. Jingles work because they are simple, easy to understand, and most of all, memorable.

Maintaining our faith in the Lord can benefit from the same principles. When God's love is simple, easy to understand and memorable we can carry it with us always.

John 3: 16 gives us the way: *"For God loved the world so much that he gave his one and only Son, so that everyone who believes in him will not perish but have eternal life."* It doesn't get any simpler than that, and it's worth remembering. And, by the way, it's been put to music.

And now, if you'll excuse me, I have an uncontrollable urge to donate a car and eat a hot dog.

Some Assembly Required

When it comes to the use of tools, my skills are legendary. By that I mean they are recognized worldwide as virtually non-existent. They are the kinds of skills that fathers strive long and hard to keep their children from developing. They are the kinds of skills that result in things like the Leaning Tower of Pisa. If my tool handling abilities were ubiquitous among the populace, IKEA would never have gotten off the ground. I remember with pride the day I completed assembling the crib for my son Evan. I pointed with great satisfaction and said, "Alright son, what are you waiting for? Get in it." He walked over, climbed over the railing and said, "Dad, it's too small." Kids! No appreciation for hard work.

I bought a new office chair for use here in the office and groaned as I opened up the box. So many pieces for such a small chair. Ah, but the instruction manual (all 10 pages of it) said in big letters "EASY INSTRUCTIONS, NO MORE 'HUH?' MOMENTS". What had I to fear? Well, plenty. By Step 2 I was no longer sure if I was reading the English, French or Spanish version of the instructions. Interestingly there wasn't much difference between them. They were all Sanskrit to me. As promised, there were no "huh?" moments, but there were a lot of "What the..." incidents. The pictures provided looked nothing like my chair, but after I reversed the position of the bottom and switched the arms a couple of times, it did begin to take shape. My favorite moments are the ones when the instructions tell you "Do NOT tighten the screws completely" right after you've tightened the screws completely.

Now I'm sitting in the chair as I write this, but I can't shake the uneasy feeling that any moment I'm going to be on the floor looking up. All day I've had this feeling that I missed step 6 in the instructions. On the positive side, I did not have any parts left over. Now for me that's a true "huh?" moment. I married my wife (in part) because she can read instructions and use tools.

Why do I do it? Why do I continue to take on projects that are simply not in the skill set that the good Lord chose to give me? I take to heart the promise that God will give us what we need to do His will. Why do I make the mistake of thinking it's God's will that I assemble furniture? Knowing and understanding the gifts that each of us is given can make the difference between being happy and being frustrated. Jesus was a carpenter. I am not. I strive to do the things that God has planned for me, and I notice that when I do I am successful. But when I take on tasks for which I am ill suited, failure is often the result.

And now, if you'll excuse me, there's a bookcase waiting for me to assemble, and I need to write an online review for the chair, if it would just stop wobbling long enough for me to type.

What Would You Do?

As if it weren't enough that we have to be concerned about the NSA, FBI, CIA, TSA and other 3 letter designated agencies monitoring our every move, now the networks are watching us as well. ABC News airs a show called "What Would You Do?" In this show, unsuspecting people are subjected to all manner of temptations from finding a bag of money on the sidewalk, to a parent verbally abusing an overweight youngster in a restaurant.

The goal of the show is to expose how ordinary people deal with legal and moral challenges in the course of their daily lives. While there are occasional uplifting moments when we see someone doing the right thing, the bulk of the program shows most people either ignoring or taking advantage of someone else's misfortune.

There are some who might say I'm a picky eater. Now, of course, they are exaggerating what is nothing more than a desire for consistent quality, and near perfection in meal time planning and execution, but somehow that minor quirk in my personality has resulted in my becoming the designated grocery shopper. On an average shopping day I will usually visit at least 3 different grocery stores. Sometimes it's because a store just doesn't carry the brand I want, and sometimes it's just that one store heavily discounts a favorite item.

I was on store #3 recently and was unloading the cart into my trunk. Being an excessively "neat" packer of plastic sacks, I paused a moment when I noticed a bag of salad mix on a lower shelf of the cart not properly seated in a sack. But this was store #3 and I was tired, so I tossed it into the trunk. It was only as I was pulling into my garage that I realized the reason the salad wasn't in a bag was that I had forgotten to pay for it when zipping through the self-checkout line.

What would you do? It would have been easy to just ignore it, but something just wouldn't let me enjoy the salad that night. For reasons that are not important I couldn't go back to the store that evening, but the next day, I found myself at the customer service center in the store handing them $2.50 (it was on sale) for the bag of salad. I'm not sure they knew exactly how to process it, but that, at least, wasn't my problem.

I wasn't afraid of the NSA or any of the other agencies that probably caught my error on a hidden camera or two, and to be perfectly honest, I wasn't really afraid of God's retribution. After all, God will forgive us our sins. I just kept thinking, "What if that money was owed to me?" Doing the right thing, no matter how small, is what being a Christian is all about.

And now, if you will excuse me, I'm debating what to do with that plate of brownies I found in the church office this morning. What would you do?

Patience is a virtue - at least my wife says it is

I'm not a patient person. If you have any doubt of that, just ask my wife. I've been on many spiritual retreats where you are asked to come to the altar and deposit your cares, concerns and sins. Inevitably, I join a long line of people and mutter to myself "Why is everyone taking so long", while I wait for my opportunity to ask the Lord to give me patience.

When I order something online (as I frequently do) or am expecting a repair part for some device or other, I eagerly await the arrival of the all-important "tracking number". Yes, I know, the notice always says it may take 24 hours for tracking information to appear, but that can't prevent my immediate visit to UPS, Fedex, or the dreaded USPS to see just where my package is currently located.

Christmas is impossible for me, and frustrating for my wife. I seem to have a sixth sense about gifts, and can't resist needing to know what's in those brightly wrapped packages under the tree. In my house, I have actually been prohibited from even "shaking" the boxes. She, who must be obeyed, has decreed there would be a "no touch" policy.

Want to know just how impatient I am? When I see a coupon for a new product in the Sunday newspaper, I instantly begin pestering the local stores wanting to know just when it will be available. I'm convinced that customer service counters throughout the county are warned about me (I could swear that was my picture on the wall in the local Safeway)..

As I sit in my office each day looking out over the construction of the new Ministry Center which is being dedicated today, I admit to a certain impatience waiting for major progress to be visible.

Over the past months, I've rejoiced when the foundation was poured, smiled when the external shell began to take shape, felt a tinge of excitement as the roof and exterior sections were filled in, and you can only imagine my excitement when the brickwork was completed. Then, as work moved to the interior of the building, I found myself needing to wander over periodically to enjoy the exhilaration of visualizing what the interior would look like when the drywall was up. This week, that became a reality.

Still, I don't think I'm alone in feeling impatient with the many changes in the promised completion date. When something you want and have been working towards for so long seems so close, it's difficult being patient.

Romans 8: 24 - 25 says: *24 For in hope we were saved. Now hope that is seen is not hope. For who hopes for what is seen? 25 But if we hope for what we do not see, we wait for it with patience.* All things in God's good time.

And now, if you'll excuse me, there's a package at the front door that needs shaking.

"The Better to See You With, My Dear"

The pastor at my church recently underwent cataract surgery. And it was very successful. I know this because a day or two after the surgery he came into the office, took one look at me and said, "Dan, I had no idea you were this good looking." Clearly (no pun intended) he was seeing much better than he had in years.

I bring up cataract surgery only because, as it turns out, I am scheduled for it myself this coming Wednesday. I have been very fortunate in my life. Other than tonsils when I was very young, and some minor knee surgery, I have not had to face many serious challenges to my health. And there was that ice cream that came with the tonsillectomy. I didn't get ice cream after knee surgery, but I'm kind of hoping that Pat will suspend our diet following the eye surgery long enough for a stopover at Carvel's.

Now even though cataract surgery is remarkably safe, and has a success rate well above 95%, I don't harbor any unrealistic expectations (will the pastor look any better?), but I do have the promise of better distance vision (it will be safe to get back on the road with me again.) The surgery itself is quite remarkable. I was able to watch a video (where would the world be without YOU TUBE?) which showed the actual procedure in real time. Two things amazed me. The first was the skill of the surgeon, but the second was the awesome design of the human eye. The human eye alone, is more than proof of a higher power at work.

While no one looks forward to surgery, I am at ease with the prospect, yes, because I have confidence in the surgeon, but mostly because I have confidence in the protection I receive from my relationship with Jesus. I don't just believe, I know, that He will be with me during this process, and that His plans for me include the need for this operation. I am confident that I will emerge equipped to serve Him even more than I can now. God is the source of it all - the gift of vision, the surgeon's skilled hands - all that we are and have comes from Him.

Lest you wonder, I am human, and I fully intend to milk this surgery for whatever period of time I can. No heavy lifting, no bending, rest, quiet, meals provided, you name it. And I'll be using the tried and true "sympathy" method. So if you feel the urge to bake brownies, or chocolate chip cookies, or you want to drop a sundae off at the church office, please feel free to do so.

And now, if you'll excuse me, I need to see if home delivery of ice cream is covered by my health insurance as a medical necessity.

How many pairs of glasses does it take to change a light bulb?

Step 1: Knowing exactly where the ladder is located, I carry it inside in order to confront the oft ridiculed task of changing a light bulb in a ceiling fixture. No glasses required.

Step 2: I go to that mysterious box in the closet that holds my stash of light bulbs. Immediately, I realize that I can't read the wattage on the bulbs, and so reach for my close-up glasses.

Step 3: I remove the close-up glasses in order to see where I'm going, and to safely climb the ladder.

Step 4: I can't quite see the little thumb screws that hold the cover on the light fixture, and so I don my mid-range glasses.

Step 5. Cover removed, I nimbly switch to my close-up glasses to check the wattage of the bulb I'm replacing.

Step 6: Someone enters the room and asks what I'm doing. I quickly remove the close-up glasses so that I can see who goes with the voice. It's my wife, Pat.

Step 7: Years of experience allow me to twist the bulb into the socket without looking at all. Glasses at the ready, though, just in case.

Step 8: Mid-range glasses on to replace the cover and thumb screws.

Step 9: Glasses off to stand back and admire my project.

You have just been witness to a strange oddity I like to call the "spectacle shuffle." It comes with age, and as a by-product of cataract surgery that greatly improved my distance vision, but may prove a boon to the over-the-counter reading glasses industry. Maintaining the right focus as we get older is difficult.

Maintaining the right focus in life, however is easy. So long as we follow the teachings of Jesus, and keep our focus on living as He would have us live, we will always find the right path. No glasses required.

And now, if you'll excuse me, Wal-Mart is having a sale on designer reading glasses.

Apology Not Accepted

Retail sales are down. Stores are cutting back on employees. Internet merchandisers are threatening the survival of brick and mortar stores. Businesses are begging for customers, and yet it seems they have nothing to sell.

Now despite what many others might want you to believe, I am an easy-going person with simple needs. I just like things to work and be as advertised. I enjoy the Sunday advertisements, and rejoice when I see something I've been wanting advertised at a great price at a local store. Whether it's an expensive piece of electronics, or nothing more than a two for one deal on mayonnaise, it's exciting to think you can get what you want at a bargain price. Yet, for some reason, stores feel absolutely no obligation to actually stock the items they advertise.

I weep thinking about all the egg salad, tuna, and BLT sandwiches that have gone uneaten because the local grocery store was out of that two for one mayo deal; or the cold stares I've received when I tried to explain to my wife that she was getting the Bed Bath and Beyond gift card for her birthday because that designer purse she wanted was "out of stock" at Lord & Taylor.

Sears advertised a chain saw for sale at a great price (I know, what is this guy doing buying a chain saw?) It was a Consumer Reports' "Best Buy". I was at the store first thing in the morning, only to be told, "Sorry sir, it's out of stock." A lamp I wanted at Lowe's was prominently displayed, but there was no stock to be found on the shelves. I found it on Amazon with the ominous warning "Only 1 Left in Stock - Hurry". I hurried, but by the time I had clicked "buy now", it was gone.

I wonder how in this age of barcodes, merchandise can ever be out of stock. One of the key benefits of barcodes is that they track sales of an item and can alert the store when supplies are running low. It's called bait and switch when a store advertises one thing then tries to sell you something more expensive with the news that the original item is sold out. Or perhaps it's just bad stock management. Either way the situation is always accompanied by a stock apology. Well, apology not accepted.

Promises, it seems, are made to be broken in the retail business. But there is one promise made to us which we never need to doubt. The promise made by Jesus to us that if we believe in Him, our sins will be forgiven and we will dwell in His house forever. No bait and switch, no limited time offers, just the Son of God's enduring word to His children. And further, with God, that familiar phrase "quantities limited" does not apply.

And now, if you'll excuse me, my rain check on mayonnaise expires today, and there's a naked tuna sandwich waiting in the fridge.

Thinking Clearly?

Having just completed successful cataract surgery, you're probably expecting that my "observations" this week will be considerably more *insightful* than usual. Fear not. They were working on correcting my vision, but did nothing to improve the mental acuity needed for such a grand turn of events.

One of my pet peeves, (I know, I know, it's hard keeping track of all of them - I use a spreadsheet), is the incredible arrogance sometimes displayed by the human race. We bipeds think that just because we can build roads, cut tunnels through mountains, develop organized societies and resurrect Twinkies that makes us masters of the planet. If you look closely at the lowly ant, that species can do almost all of the same things (with the possible exception of resurrecting Twinkies.)

We are amazing creations, and we have been given the ability to think, to plan, to build, and to dream. Some of the things we have planned and built have been remarkable, others we might prefer to forget (think leisure suits and congress). But for all of our power, all of our skill, the planet does occasionally remind us that our power is limited. In the face of hurricanes, tornadoes, tsunamis, wildfires and other natural events, we suddenly realize we are no more powerful than are those lowly ants we look down upon.

We humans have made great medical and technical advances. We have made it possible to feed millions, to irrigate deserts, and to send astronauts to the moon. We can restore sight to aging eyes, replace defective organs, and so much more. And yes, we have developed monstrous weapons of mass destruction.

We may well have the capability of annihilating ourselves, but I do not believe we can end life on this planet. When I listen to those who would suggest we have that power, my arrogance alarm is triggered.

Proverbs 25: 6 – 7 refers to the sin of pride. The human race has much to be proud of, but we should never forget that our successes and accomplishments come not from our efforts alone, but are made possible by the gifts God has granted to us, and the foundations of life that He has put into place.

As President Obama once said, "You didn't build that." Perhaps he too was reminding us that we are all executing the plans of the "master builder".

And now, if you'll excuse me, I need to get to the grocery store. My supply of Hostess products is nearly depleted.

And the Survey Says...

According to a recent survey (of people who have enough time on their hands to respond to surveys), stepping on a crack really will break your mother's back. That's right, a survey of recent immigrants from the Amazon Rain Forest confirms that old myth that has kept me from walking comfortably on sidewalks since the age of 4. This was authenticated by the fact that of those surveyed whose mothers had in fact broken their backs, virtually all of their children had at one time or another stepped on a crack. Case closed.

We live in an age where I sometimes think our lives are ruled, or at least directed, by the innumerable surveys the results of which are constantly thrown at us. Pick up a newspaper today and you may find a survey showing that it is likely Democrats will pick up the House of Representatives. Pick up the newspaper tomorrow, and there may well be a survey showing just the opposite. I'm told it's all in how you ask the question.

Remember that popular daytime game show, "Family Feud"? You know, that show where the question might be something like "Name a planet you can recognize just by looking at it." Answer: "The Moon." The "survey" actually awarded 3 points for that answer.

Questions can be designed to manipulate us. Consider salespeople; they are often masters at asking questions that get you in the habit of saying "yes." "Do you want your children to have financial security?" "Wouldn't you want your family to eat healthy?" "Would you like to have less pain in your life?" Now, I might well answer, "No, I enjoy a little pain now and then." And I might possibly say, "No, if my kids want financial security they can work for it." But, let's face it, most of us would probably say yes to those questions.

Discerning fact from fiction, truth from myth, can be very difficult in today's world. Actress Clara Peller in a famous ad from Wendy's once asked "Where's the beef?" That phrase became a common way of asking where the substance was in a statement. It was often in reference to politicians' proposals. It's still relevant today when assessing the value of surveys or other statements of popular belief.

As Christians, we know where the "beef" is. The substance of our beliefs can be found in the Word of God, the Bible. In particular the New Testament. No surveys, no oddball questions, no popular myths, just straight talk about the Son of God who came to save man from his sins. If only the word of man were as reliable as the promise of Jesus Christ, what a world we would have.

And now, if you'll excuse me, I have some patching to do on the sidewalk outside of my home. A lot of children with mothers will be passing by and their backs are in my hands.

Where Are the Opposable Thumbs?

I am a huge fan of science fiction no matter how you spell it, "sci-fi", "sy-fy" it's all great to me. I was "Trekking" long before William Shatner started doing weight loss commercials. I have a copy of the script of *The Trouble With Tribbles* (one of the most popular episodes from the original *Star Trek* TV series). I read the classic *Starship Troopers* by Robert A. Heinlein when I was 12, and have watched the movie version so often that I've gotten a backup DVD just in case.

And don't even get me started on *Doctor Who*. If you've seen my desk in the church office, you noticed, I'm sure, the Dalek guarding the computer, and the TARDIS USB port (sorry, no time to explain these - that's what Google is for.)

I understand perfectly well the suspension of disbelief concept that applies when watching a movie or reading a book, but I also sometimes wonder if the writers, directors and producers ever consider the absurdity of their design choices.

You see, I have a problem with the depiction of most aliens on television and in the movies. The poor things never have opposable thumbs. Take this one from *Doctor Who* (please). He's called a Slitheen, and he's (well I think he's a he) a really great character, but how in the world he was able to build and pilot a spaceship, much less operate complicated gear with small buttons, is never quite explained. Putting on protective goggles would be a life threatening task. How could the Alien from *Alien* ever have gotten off its home planet (where would you even find a helmet to fit that head?)

In my opinion, these improbable and unworkable body designs look much more like the product of random evolution than anything we would find here on Earth. Molecules floating around in space that just happen to come together at some point to create a life form, it seems to me, would be much more likely to resemble a confusing mass of unrelated and non-functioning parts like the Slitheen.

When we look at the beauty, the complexity, the careful integration of elements that go into making a man or a woman, we can see clearly the touch of the Master's hand. Whatever building blocks God started with, human kind was not a result of random assembly, or trial and error. God designed and planned each perfect element. As Shakespeare wrote, "What a piece of work is man!" What a masterful God is ours.

And now, if you'll excuse me, I'm designing a three-fingered alien that can play the guitar.

Hurry Up and Wait!

"Thank you for calling the Acme Defibrillator customer support line. Your call is very important to us. All available associates are busy helping other customers. You are number 6, 213 in the queue. Average wait time is 3 days 24 minutes." Sound familiar? No doubt you've had a similar experience. I'm convinced the "single" customer service rep that companies actually employ represent the most overworked folks in the world. Still, it's just one of many examples of our 21st century hurry up and wait society. Yesterday, I visited a doctor's office, and found myself languishing silently in that room I call the "Land that time forgot." You know, that place where you are told to sit in a flimsy open backed gown, without a single piece of reading material; that place where you are told "The Doctor will be with you shortly." I'm convinced the doctor is on hold trying to reach the Acme Defibrillator Company.

As fast as computers are at processing, it seems like we spend an awful lot of time waiting for them to complete some task or another: waiting for Windows updates to download; waiting for them to install; waiting for antivirus definitions to update; waiting for programs to load; waiting for the system to restart. Some days I find myself covered with cobwebs waiting for my fast machine to do something. Pat says it's a good look for me.

Whether it's waiting for seats in a crowded restaurant, watching the mailbox for that special package to arrive, waiting for the laundry to finish so that you can wear your favorite outfit or just waiting for dinner to be ready, our patience is constantly tested.

I'm a gadget nut. I've got dozens of them, but I can't resist the allure of the newest to hit the market. For my birthday this year, I had hinted to my wife (that means I sent her an email with a picture, price and the places it could be found) that I wanted a ROKU 3 streaming player. It was weeks before my birthday, and I was impatient. I was forced to try to divert my attention with my computer, my Kindle Fire HD, the 250 channels on my FIOS TV, my smartphone, my Blu-Ray player and one or two devices the names of which I cannot even remember. But my thoughts were always of the gadget to come.

Life today demands that we learn to wait patiently. That's not an easy thing for most of us. Imagine the patience that is required of our Lord as He waits for His children to follow the path set out for them by His Son. How far back in the list of priorities for us is obedience to God? Are we patient as we await answers to our prayers? Do we look forward to Sunday worship with the same sense of excitement we show for the next gadget to come along? Patience is a virtue, I've heard.

And now, if you'll excuse me, Acme Defibrillator's hold system is playing my favorite song.

Which Way is Up?

I consider myself a fairly intelligent person (some opinions may differ), yet I am completely inept when it comes to solving simple everyday problems. Take the heat shield for my car's windshield ("please", as Henny Youngman might say.) A simple yet elegant solution to an overheating car interior in the summertime. In the words of a popular Geico spokesman, "So simple a caveman could do it." But let's face it, you can never find a caveman when you need one. My attempts to open and set up one of those things might be mistaken for a mad man wrestling an alligator in the front seat of his car. Once unfolded, I couldn't get the silly thing to stay up in the window. It kept falling down. Oh sure, just pull down the visors you're thinking - simple, right. Yea, simple if you know you're supposed to do that.

I can handle complex computer software, but I can't figure out how to get one of those hermetically wrapped cheese snack sticks open. I have visions of being found dead on a desert island one day, surrounded by boxes of the devilish things.

One of my favorite pastimes is assembling boxed furniture (please ignore the crowd of skeptics laughing uproariously in the background). I once assembled a bookcase in such a way that it ended up looking like a telephone stand (why do manufacturers include more pieces than you actually need?).

That's why I married my wife, Pat. Not only can she assemble boxed furniture, but she was actually able to take that telephone stand and turn it into a six drawer desk.

Turns out it's true. God does indeed give each of us unique skills and abilities. And one of the keys to being happy and content is realizing that you can't do everything yourself. Pat often needs help with technology, and so we have an understanding. I'll fix her computer, and she'll do all of the furniture assembly. While I might wish I had some of her skills, God knew what I needed, and saw to it that I would find her. We complement each other, and God provides whatever we may be lacking. Life is good - with God.

And now, if you'll excuse me, I have to try to figure out why the front door won't open. Push? Pull? Can't they put a sign on it?.

Dan learns that "fixing" isn't all it's cracked up to be.

As my wife would be quick to confirm, I am a huge fan of a daily comic strip called "Pearls Before Swine", drawn by Stephan Pastis. The characters are animals, but their life experiences are often strangely close to my own.

Now here's a revelation you've probably never heard before: men and women look at things differently. I know, I know, it's shocking. The seemingly innocuous question, "How was your day?" elicits quite different responses from men and women (I am generalizing here, I know there are exceptions). In my home, I generally offer a lengthy response to this question, e.g. "OK." or "Pretty good." On a really exciting day I might go so far as to say, "Not bad." I think I'm like a lot of men in that I tend to put work behind me once the day is over.

My wife Pat, on the other hand, prefers to provide a bit more detail. She has to work with government agencies and their bureaucracies and that sometimes results in frustration. She needs to vent. It's my keen ability to *not* sense this sort of thing that often gets me into trouble. You see, like many men, I see my role as a fixer, a remover of roadblocks. As she describes her day, at the first sign of a problem I'm ready to leap in with a "solution." I underestimate her need to just vent.

Turns out I'm much like Pig in the Pearls strip. I mistakenly think my job is to eliminate the problem, and therefore the need to vent. This error in judgment has led to many breakable objects being thrown my way.

How marvelous our God is to listen quietly to all of His children as they pour out their frustrations daily to Him. How patient and understanding He must be. And when we are finished, God, in His infinite wisdom and generosity, often provides the real "fix" that is needed.

And now, if you'll excuse me, I'm working on my own version of the Serenity Prayer: God, grant me the serenity to listen quietly when my wife needs to vent, the courage to resist the urge to fix those things which do not ask to be fixed, and the wisdom to know when to shut up.

The Day the Music Died

If beautiful music that had partnered with your morning coffee to bring a bit of sunshine into your days for more than two decades suddenly stopped - would you notice?

A dear member of the family passed away last week, and I didn't notice. His name was Webster. He was smart, active, colorful, and best of all, he could make beautiful music. And he did this for more than 24 years. Each morning as Pat and I raced to make coffee, grab the morning paper and prepare for the day, Webster would begin his serenade. It was an eclectic collection of tunes ranging from Tchaikovsky's "1812 Overture" (or at least part of it), to familiar Christmas carols (regardless of the month.) But that was OK. Webster was, after all, a Cockatiel.

But last Thursday, the music died. Webster had stopped singing. I made the coffee, read the paper, dressed and went to work, and I had not noticed what was missing. I had not noticed the absence of his music. I had not noticed the absence of his chatter (he would always greet me with "Hello, Webster".) I had not noticed the silence. I had not noticed that our friend was gone. It fell to my wife Pat to convey the news to me. She was his best friend, and the one who fed, watered, and kept his living area clean.

As much as I will miss the pleasure this little creature brought into our lives, I am almost more distressed by how quickly he left this world without my even noticing. As I did every morning, I was sitting just a few feet from him, blithely drinking coffee and reading the paper. I should have noticed the sound of silence, but I didn't. Some might say Webster was only a bird, but they would be wrong. He was so much more. He was light, love and song. He was a gift from God that brightened our lives.

How is it that we can go about our daily lives so engrossed in our own routines, our own business that we fail to notice important things happening around us? We take for granted every day the people, animals and things with which God has blessed us. God surrounds us with wonderful things that bless our lives. How often do we remember to acknowledge them?

Tomorrow, and every morning, when I arise, I will try to remember the people, places and things that are important to me. The things I love and will miss when they are gone. And I will thank the Lord for each and every one of them.

And now, if you'll excuse me, I have a wife to hug, and a fuzzy dog to kiss (or maybe I should reverse that.)

My Dog Went to the Maryland DogFest, and All I Got Was...

It's easy to tell that Father's Day has long passed, and my birthday is still a few weeks away. How do I know this? Well, I'm back to playing second fiddle to a Morkie (that's a Maltese/Yorkie mix) whose name is Darby. Of course, to many in the theater-going world, he's better known as Chowsie for his role in "Gypsy". To others he's known as the winner of this year's Sunday Maryland DogFest Best Costume Contest. He's been called (subjective opinions I know) the cutest dog in Charles County. Darby is constantly surrounded by adoring fans of the female persuasion. He bats his eyes and they swoon. I bat my eyes, and they hand me a tissue and an allergy pill.

Most recently he's gaining fame as the World War II Flying Ace bravely carrying the mail to the Glory Days Antique Center in Newburg. Whether or not he has dreams (do dogs dream?) of being a fighter pilot, he takes to wearing the helmet, goggles, and bomber jacket as if they were a normal part of his daily routine.

He has many other outfits. As a matter of fact, it's been suggested by someone wearing an expensive ring on her left hand, that I might want to consider vacating my walk-in-closet in our bedroom to make room for a shorter member of the family with a much more extensive wardrobe than mine. My wife Pat is a costumer and seamstress, and her skills roughly break down as follows: 50% costuming for theater; 49% costuming for Darby; 1% repair/alterations for husband.

Darby is the most compliant creature I know. He calmly accepts trying on and wearing whatever outfit Pat creates for him. He sits quietly while she stretches his arms into a traditional Scottish kilt (complete with sporan and Glengarry hat); he hardly squirms when being transformed into the title character from the classic Disney movie "Darby O'Gill and the Little People" which includes a jacket, scarf and mandatory Irish cap. Wearing the goggles of an aviator can't be comfortable for a dog, but Darby does it willingly. Perhaps he really enjoys dressing up, but I think it's more likely that he simply trusts that he is loved, and that the person he loves in return would never do anything to hurt or harm him.

We have that same trust in our Lord. Sometimes He will ask us to do things with which we are not comfortable, but we know He loves us and would never do anything to hurt or harm us. It's called trust.

And now, if you'll excuse me, I need to find the sewing kit. I've lost another button, and the local seamstress is busy working on a Renaissance outfit for a small Morkie.

Blazing Sun, Flip Flops, Chlorine - Not Quite Heaven

I have every hope and promise of one day visiting long lost loved ones in Heaven, but this past weekend I was given a glimpse of what might be waiting for me should I end up going in the other direction. It was Father's Day, and my wonderful daughter, who normally takes after me, called to invite Pat and me to a place even the NSA would never think to look for me - a private swim club (think blazing sun and flip flops. everywhere.) You see, I don't swim. I never have. Now it would be easy to attribute my lack of interest in pool activities to my less than Adonis-like appearance in a bathing suit, but it's a bit more complicated than that. Let's just say I had a very bad experience as a young child at the hands of an Aunt who thought the pool was a good way to teach someone who wouldn't do as he was told a lesson. It worked. And I haven't been in a pool since.

But I wasn't going to let a little thing like bathing attire stop me from being with my daughter and granddaughter on Father's Day - and besides, I've lost a "little" weight on this diet of mine (I can now actually button my jeans - and just the other day, I SAW MY TOES! How cool is that?) As I rummaged through my dresser looking for a bathing suit I came across the last one I wore. It was on my honeymoon with Pat, and the one and only time I ever wore a Speedo (children - hide your eyes.) So I did what any man my age would do, I fired up the computer and scoured the Internet searching for just the right look guaranteed to embarrass my daughter. I found it at Kohls - and even had a 20% off coupon.

And so, armed with hats, minimal pride and a cooler full of snacks, Pat and I headed to the swim club. Expecting to be conspicuous, I was delighted to see that Kohls had apparently had a very good sales week. I recognized a lot of the attire the other men were wearing - ha, but I'll bet they didn't get 20% off, I smugly chuckled to myself. One of life's little victories, I suppose.

But here's the part that I really like. Neither my daughter nor granddaughter looked twice at what I was wearing. It didn't matter to them. Little Emma was delighted to play with the hats that Pat and I were wearing, and nobody seemed to care that I never got into the pool. We were all just glad to be together.

Families understand us, and they accept us just the way we are (OK, maybe not the neon orange swim trunks.) We fathers love our children, and want nothing more than that they love us back. Our Heavenly Father is no different. He loves us just as He has made us, and asks only that we love and honor Him in return.

And now, if you'll excuse me, I'm going to try to return a barely used neon orange swim suit.

Greater love hath no man than this, that he should peel a hard boiled egg for his wife.

With humble apologies to John 15:13

Now to be clear, I've never carried my wife from a burning building, or resuscitated her after rescuing her from a raging river. I've never fought off a gang of toughs trying to steal her purse, nor have I even driven off a Fuller Brush Man about to close a big sale with her. But unlike those obvious deeds of courage and selflessness I have performed the ultimate act of love by peeling hard boiled eggs for Pat's lunch. Those who may scoff at this feat are those who have never suffered the agony of an inedible eggshell that is wed eternally to the edible interior.

OK, OK, already, I know in the pantheon of problems, this may not seem worthy of an entire column, but in the realm of life's little frustrations, it is right up there with "an unwatched pot boils immediately", and "the easiest way to find something lost around the house is to buy a replacement."

Granted my egg peeling technique may be a bit heavy handed at times. My usual approach is what I call the "smash and roll." The results are usually not pretty, but there is a certain satisfaction in showing the egg that I'm stronger than it is. Apparently the problem is all my fault. According to the experts (who knew there were experts on hard boiled eggs?). I should never buy fresh eggs, and I should leave them out of the refrigerator overnight before cooking. So, the key, I guess, is to use stale and bacteria prone eggs in order to facilitate peeling. It's comforting to know that I'll have easy to peel eggs that may kill me. I have developed a new found respect for the poor chicks who have to battle their way out of their incredible prisons in order to see the light of day.

Peeling a hard boiled egg for someone you love, filling their car with gas (just because you care), watching a romantic comedy (when you know full well there's a zombie flick on HBO), or just giving that special someone a hug when they come home, all of these little gestures say "I love you." God won't do those little things for us, but He is constantly showering each of us with expressions of His love: waking up in the morning to a beautiful sunrise; enjoying a meal; blessing us with healthy children; allowing us to use the gifts and talents He has given to us. Greater love has no person than that which God has for each us. And that trumps any frustration.

And now, if you'll excuse me, on the guarantee that they would peel perfectly, I "cooked" some hard boiled eggs in the oven last night, and I can't wait to watch the shells just melt right off.

Where Have All the Neckties Gone?

With apologies to Pete Seeger, Peter, Paul & Mary, The Kingston Trio and anyone else who ever sang "Where Have All the Flowers Gone?"

Father's Day has changed. There's no doubt about that. The days of dad excitedly tearing open the present wrapped by tiny hands (or perhaps a loving wife), only to find another...tie, are drawing to a close. No one wears them much anymore. This demise of a once beloved male accoutrement prompted me to unscrupulously modify an also beloved folk song.

Where have all the neckties gone? Long time passing.
Where have all the neckties gone? Long time ago.
Where have all the neckties gone? Gone to funerals everyone.
When will we ever wear? When will we ever wear, them again?

Of course I know that there are still some occupations which require men to "tie the knot" (so to speak), but many places that were once bastions of good dress codes have drifted towards the dark side (think casual Friday).

I wore a coat and tie throughout most of my life, beginning with my first job in the plumbing department of Sears - yes we wore a tie while selling greasy pipe fittings to customers. The bulk of my career was spent in environments that more resembled "Dilbert's" workspace than anything else. I think my tie even looked like his once or twice. In fact, I probably own 50 or more ties right now. I just don't have the occasion to wear them very often - although there is that occasional funeral. I wonder, if asked, how many young boys would be able to tie a tie?

We've become a much more casual society. Shorts, sweat pants, and even the dreaded flip flops are considered acceptable in many situations. Most restaurants will take you anyway you are dressed. Even church has become a place where casual dress is welcome.

We're mixed up about what works and what doesn't. Young men often seem unable to make up their minds, and so will wear a shirt, a tie, and a pair of jeans, or is this just another in a series of modern trends that I missed?

It's true, God doesn't love us more because we wear a suit and tie to church. But the way we dress does say something about how important we consider an event to be. Being casual isn't a bad thing, but knowing when to show respect for someone or something isn't either. I used to enjoy getting home from work and saying, "Now I can change clothes and relax." Often, I don't need to change anymore. I sort of miss that, just a little.

So, since ties are out, what do you give a dad who means the world to you? It's easy; give him a hug, a kiss, tell him you love him and thank God he is yours.

Nature to Dan: "Drop the camera, step away from the woods and no one will get hurt!"

It's an idyllic day. The sun is shining, a cool breeze is blowing. Birds are singing, and the landscape seems positively overflowing with life. And so it is that I am once again lulled into thinking I can step confidently into the realm of natural wonders. Armed with nothing more than my Canon (zoom, macro, and other lenses), and a complete aura of obliviousness surrounding me, I ventured into THE WOODS.

Although n a frequency far outside my ability to hear, I am convinced that my first step tripped an alarm that every other living thing in the forest heard instantly.

Warning! Warning! Proximity Alert!
Unauthorized city dweller with camera approaching!

And much as the minutemen responded to the cries of Paul Revere by taking up arms against the invading British, so too did the forest shift to a posture of offense. The trees grew angry, dropping leaves, nuts, and other debris as I passed. The ground beneath my feet grew wet and slippery, and I sensed I was sinking lower with each new step. Roots seemed to rise up out of nowhere to snare my spotless white walking shoes. Creatures with six or more legs were making their way up past the scant protection of my socks. Others were latching onto my unprotected arms and neck determined to lower my red blood cell count. I was becoming part of the food chain, but no longer was I at the top of that pyramid. The sun beat down mercilessly, (yes, there is sun in the forest) converting my once pleasing skin tones into shades resembling hot house tomatoes. And from the wildlife? Not a peep. A water snake slithering by in a small pond was the only sign of life in this wilderness. Oh, yes, there was that bird who flew overhead and...well you get the picture.

No, this wasn't a scene from a low budget SyFy channel movie about a planet gone mad. This was simply a standard visit to the outdoors by someone who occasionally needs to be reminded that nature is no place for a tech savvy city boy.

God equips each of us to do the work he has planned for us. As we grow in our faith and relationship with Christ, we learn to use the skills we've been given, and not long for the ones we do not possess. The forest is not the place for me.

And now, if you'll excuse me, nature calls, but this time it's indoors and I know what to do.

Is this medication right for me?

Do you love your doctor? Actually I love mine, but I don't think the feeling is mutual. I get the impression he may be trying to avoid me. I don't know if doctors give their receptionists a list of those patients they'd rather not see, but I'm convinced my name is on a sticky note right next to the phone in my doctor's office. The routine is predictable. I call; the receptionist politely tells me there's nothing available for the next six months and asks if I would be willing to see one of the good doctor's assistants. Now I have nothing against physician's assistants, I'm sure they're more than competent, but I simply must see the doctor himself. The receptionist knows this because when she asks what my problem is, I always tell her the same thing. I heard about 72 medications, and I need to know if one of them might be right for me.

The advertising for new drugs is amazing. It frequently manages to convince me that I have health problems I often didn't even know existed. "Are you feeling tired?" Well, yes. "Are you constantly craving sweets?" Well, yes. "Is your hair losing its luster?" Well, you already know about my follicle problem. "Are you pregnant or nursing?" Whew, well at least I can say no to that one - although the commercial makes me feel like I should be doing one or the other. No matter, the latest medication has all the answers, but you must "Check with your doctor to see if (insert medication here) is right for you." What's a sensible fellow to do? What if I don't check, and I miss an important medication that is *right* for me?

A few years ago I had minor knee surgery, and during one of the follow-up visits with the doctor, I mentioned that I was having some arthritic pain in my fingers and hands. He gave me two sample packets of an arthritis medication that he said would help. When I opened the package and pulled out the information sheet, the very first line was printed in bold face in a font 5 times the size of the rest of the sheet. It read: **MAY CAUSE DEATH**. Now if there was ever a need for an exclamation point it was after that statement, but no, just a period. I stood there for a moment, glass of water at the ready, and mentally weighed the two alternatives: less pain, DEATH, less pain, DEATH. I had a glass of wine and threw the medicine in the trash.

While modern medicine is a wonderful thing, I am always frightened by the number of warnings and disclaimers that accompany every advertisement (it's that little voice speaking quietly in the background while happy looking people cavort on sailboats or beaches.) When we look to ourselves for solutions we accept the risk of side effects and unintended consequences. But when we seek God's guidance through prayer and rely on His wisdom to direct us, we never need worry about the fine print.

And now, if you'll excuse me, I need to get back to calling my doctor. I added two new medications to my list after watching TV last night.